The Ukrainian Tarot

Flower of the Magic Fern

TANIA ANDRUSHKO

www.taniaandrushko.com

4880 Lower Valley Road, Atglen, PA 19310

Copyright © 2025 by Tania Andrushko

Library of Congress Control Number: 2024952901

All rights reserved. No part of this work may be reproduced or used in any form or by any means—graphic, electronic, or mechanical, including photocopying or information storage and retrieval systems—without written permission from the publisher.

The scanning, uploading, and distribution of this book or any part thereof via the Internet or any other means without the permission of the publisher is illegal and punishable by law. Please purchase only authorized editions and do not participate in or encourage the electronic piracy of copyrighted materials.

"Red Feather Mind Body Spirit" logo is a trademark of Schiffer Publishing, Ltd.
"Red Feather Mind Body Spirit Feather" logo is a registered trademark of Schiffer Publishing, Ltd.

Cover design by Brenda McCallum
Type set in Cinzel / Times New Roman
ISBN: 978-0-7643-7017-5
Printed in China

10 9 8 7 6 5 4 3 2 1

Published by REDFeather Mind, Body, Spirit
An imprint of Schiffer Publishing, Ltd.
4880 Lower Valley Road
Atglen, PA 19310
Phone: (610) 593-1777; Fax: (610) 593-2002
Email: Info@redfeathermbs.com
Web: www.redfeathermbs.com

Ignite your Light!

*Expand your Heart in Love & Peace,
so you can inspire humanity to do the same.*

Contents

FOREWORD 7

HOW IT STARTED 9

HOW IT EVOLVED 11

HOW IT WORKS 13

HOW TO DO READINGS 17

MAJOR ARCANA 23

MINOR ARCANA

    AIR 69

    WATER 99

    FIRE 129

    EARTH 159

GRATITUDE & ACKNOWLEDGMENTS 189

A MESSAGE FROM THE ARTIST MARY 190

A MESSAGE FROM THE ARTIST OLENA 191

FOREWORD

I am who I am, and though I long denied it, my Ukrainian ancestry has haunted me my entire life.

As a child, my Baba spoke to me in broken English, but perfect Ukrainian, and the funny thing was, I could always understand her Ukrainian much better than her English, although technically, I was never formally taught. However, it would take me almost forty years to realize that the real reason I could interpret her always emotionally fed communications was that imbued within the words she was speaking was a mystical and palpable energy that exceeded her short 5-feet-nothing stature.

My Baba was just one month shy of her 102nd birthday when she transitioned, and there is still so much I want to ask her. As with many immigrants, the trauma associated with leaving your home (especially to escape war) and navigating the harshness of a new and unwelcoming land can dampen the desire to speak about anything other than the basic survival stories of a life long (but hardly) lived. Like many descendants of traumatized ancestors, I spent much of my life in avoidance of their pain . . . which ultimately blocked me from the greater realization of their (and my own) gifts.

As fate would have it, the last two years during the war in Ukraine have hit me head on, and it is as though my ancestors are speaking to me and calling me home. I have been on a journey to learn the truth of my past, and to my surprise, the medicine that my grandparents practiced and carried with them long after they left the rolling Carpathians is also alive and surging through my body.

The symbolism and sacred rituals of Ukrainian pagan culture are fantastically similar to the ancient wisdom of the Vedas (which I have studied extensively), as well as many North American Indigenous cultures (to which I feel a deep soul connection). And suddenly, everything is beginning to make sense.

The more that I uncovered, the more empowered I would become. And the more empowered I would become, the more responsible I would feel for sharing this wisdom with so many others who were also searching for the missing pieces to their own sacred line.

When I heard the first whispers of this deck, I felt every cell in my body wake up and lean in. In fact, I'm pretty sure that my excitement quickly turned to impatience, and I felt like a child waiting anxiously for Christmas to arrive.

This feels like a second chance for many of us to ask the questions that we never got the chance to ask, and to learn about another spiritually important piece of our history that seems so difficult to track down.

I feel that the timing of the release of this deck couldn't come at a more important and divine time, since Ukraine is currently under fire and many of its residents are fighting, fleeing, or taking cover. And since all of life moves in cycles, it's as if this revolution carries with it the ghosts of past wars. Many Ukrainians are refusing to forget the many tragedies of the last century and are rising together, not only in their physical strength but also in their spiritual strength.

The teachings shared here are for everyone to lean into, not only those with Ukrainian blood in their veins. This wisdom is the wisdom of the earth, the cosmos, and the gods, and what you will come to learn as you experience the Flower of the Magic Fern is how interconnected your own story is with that of the collective.

Let your own story unfold as you open your mind and your heart to the mystical guidance of this ancient wisdom.

—Mandy Trapp, medicine woman

HOW IT STARTED

On February 22, 2022, I was sitting on a beach in Costa Rica creating an earth mandala, a ritual I do when I travel. I gathered all the elements needed to start the ritual and then began to speak the desires I wished to create. I usually ask for health, prosperity, guidance, and support. This time, however, the words that came were "Peace and Love. Peace and Love for Humanity." A part of me, much deeper than I knew at the time, was asking for blessings on a much-larger scale. I shared with my husband, Yuriy, this strange and touching encounter under the Pura Vida sky. Two days later, when we returned from our travels to snowy Alberta, Canada, my native city in Ukraine was bombed.

The year that followed was full of transformation, change, grief, and discovery. Through the pain of what I was witnessing in my homeland, the war in Ukraine ignited my love for the traditions and culture that blessed my childhood. It offered (and continues to offer) me an immense amount of gratitude for the opportunities and experiences I have been gifted here in Canada. These experiences, many of which have been prompted by my need for truth and personal connection, have taken me on an uncommon journey.

In 2021, I was called to be a student of the Institute of Shamanic Medicine, British Columbia, Canada. Ukrainian friends would ask me, "Why would you take a shamanic course if you are Christian?" My shamanic classmates would ask the opposite: "Why do you go to the church on Easter if you are in shamanic class?" The answer is simple: There is only one God—and God is Love. My belief in a higher power transcends tradition and culture.

When I was in one of my shamanic sweat experiences, I received a visit by a luminous being with a clear message: "You will inspire humanity to expand in Love and Peace. You will do so by launching the first ever *Ukrainian Tarot* deck." I listened to this powerful message without hesitation. My heart said yes and my brain quickly started to imagine how I would bring all of the richness and depth of Ukrainian tradition that lives in Ukrainian hearts and souls to this divinely guided gift to humanity.

And then the magic began! Every step brought more and more synchronicities. I surrendered to the Truth, seeking to be expressed through me. I knew that one day you would be holding this box in your hands, feeling the potency of what you are about to discover.

In the creation of this deck, I cried, I laughed, I struggled, I danced with joy, and I found my Flower of the Magic Fern. This magical flower is said to bloom only once a year, on the shortest night of the year, bringing good fortune to whoever finds it. As the legend goes, this flower can be found only in the darkest of forests in Ukraine, and only if your heart and intentions are pure. Through this initiation, I found my Flower of the Magic Fern, and my hope for you is that this deck will help you find your own.

From my heart to yours,

TANIA Andrushko

HOW IT EVOLVED

Human life depends on natural phenomena, which are often recounted through mythological events. Some of the major deities for humanity were the heavenly bodies of sun and moon. These revered deities were personified in legends, and their celestial movements were incorporated into their earth-based calendars. Furthermore, various rites were invented to explain the involvement of people in the creation of the world, and their efforts to help the gods, during times of evolution and change.

The Ukrainian calendar is known as Svarog's Circle. This calendar is circular, has the four cardinal directions, and places humanity at the center.

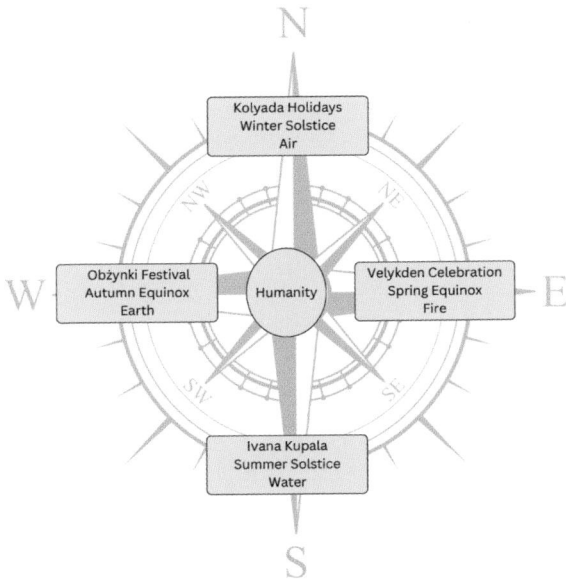

The calendar takes the form of a slender and symmetrical eight-pointed star, with four major solar holidays corresponding to each of the four solar phases (summer and winter solstices, spring and fall equinoxes). The northern aspect of the Ukrainian calendar marks the winter solstice, called Kolyada, while its opposite aspect, the southern, marks the summer cycle, known as Ivana Kupala. The eastern aspect reflects the spring cycle of Velykden, while its opposite, the autumn harvest cycle, called Obżynki, sits in the west. Our shamanic ancestors used this cyclical calendar to explain their worldview, which is reflected in the many legends told throughout this deck.

The richness of Ukrainian culture is vast, making it challenging to fit the depth of meaning into this seventy-eight-card deck. Yet, my Soul was guided and the voice of Spirit spoke clearly, describing what was meant to be shared. Beautiful colored images were inspired and created in conjunction with the stunning Ukrainian culture, spirituality, and folklore. The journey has been divinely guided from start to finish, and now I am thrilled to invite you along.

There is magic in the natural world. Yet, in this age of technology, we find ourselves easily distracted, and the treasures of ancestral wisdom can get completely overlooked. Returning to the roots of understanding of how the universe speaks to us through the spirit that lives through everything becomes an important skill. My intention is to help you, the reader, see the magic in the real world and return to the roots of understanding how the universe speaks to us. May this book help you to remember who you are and the vital role you play in this lifetime.

HOW IT WORKS

The Ukrainian Tarot: Flower of the Magic Fern is a classic seventy-eight-card Tarot deck. The structure is identical to the standard Tarot deck, with both Major and Minor Arcanas. The Major Arcana is often complex and significant, with twenty-two cards to reveal the major life events and energies that are influencing what is happening now. The Minor Arcana is presented through four elements—Air, Water, Fire, and Earth—with fourteen cards in each—Page to Ace. The role of each element is very specific, and they have their own directions on the medicine wheel, representing Intellect, Emotions, Actions, and Manifestation in the Material World.

While readings are intuitive and spirit-led, it is important to explain how all the cards are connected. The table below offers synchronicities and connections between the numbers, art, and written messages. I encourage you to trust any additional meaning that you may find in these beautiful legends and artwork. This is exactly why we have a note section underneath each card, so you can add your intuitive hits and downloads right there and then.

One of the medicines I hold is that of the Truth Teller. I invite you to be courageous to say what you are called to say. You have my permission and blessing to use this deck in the best way that serves you. I would love for you to speak your Truth with a capital "T" too! I trust that you will be divinely guided.

Page	This is a card of new beginnings. The flower shows the way to the fruits of the harvest. This fruit may be the result of a new opportunity, so we can get ready for change.
Messenger	Birds are connected to the creation of the world. Spring is brought by the wings of birds in flight. They are symbols of the victory of life over death and day over night. Birds create a cosmological model of the universe, because they are seen as messengers between the world of gods and people. With this in mind, birds represent messengers of change.

Queen	For centuries, women have played a significant role in building the history of our civilization. Women have an impact on society and its footprint within, around, and among communities. They passionately serve as connectors of people to the natural elements. Queens influence and inspire the development and formation of culture, art, education, science, literature, and many other spheres of our lives.
King	Kings are the doers of the court and represent healthy masculinity through the natural elements. They build the foundations of progress and work on development and expansion within the physical world
2	The number two {2} represents partnerships. We start in partnership with ourselves (air | mind). We then long for partnership with another human (water | feelings). Once this relationship is satisfied, we progress to community or the collective (fire | action). Finally, we arrive at the divine connection between the human and the spiritual worlds (earth | body).
3	Number three {3} implies the energy of expression and creativity. From time immemorial, the beat of a love song comes to us in ¾ time. It is the lilt of our mother's lullaby, which accompanies us throughout our lives, whether in sadness or in joy. Songs and music are special art forms that are inextricably linked with culture and history. Music, song, and sound accompany us through our lives, from birth to death, inspiring creativity and expression. Musical instruments represent the energy of expression in this category.

4	Number four {4} is a number of foundations, support, and stability. Like the legs of a stool or the corner posts of a building, there is stability in four. We all seek the grounds to stay strong and build our dreams and aspirations. The fours in this deck are represented by Ukrainian national symbols in connection with the four elements. They represent a strong foundation.
5	Number five {5} represents spiritual growth and self-confidence. It is believed that the work of the soul is produced by our hands. Our ancestors sought to create with their own hands, gaining fame and recognition for their skills in crafts such as pottery, ceramics, weaving, blacksmithing, carving, cooperage, and masonry. Competence and confidence come from careful action and love of work.
6	Number six {6} carries the energy of balance and harmony. In shamanic teachings we are taught to seek those energies in the trees. According to the beliefs of our ancestors, the souls of grandparents are in the woods, and the tree is a kind of connection between this world and the heavenly world. "As above, so below," conveys this balance and harmony and may be easily visualized in the limbs and roots of a tree.
7	Number seven {7} is a powerful number that symbolizes a person's inner wisdom, self-awareness, intuition, and mysticism. The most-sacred Ukrainian traditions and rites share the magic of seeking the path forward, with an inner knowing of the map. The concept of the mystic and intuition is conveyed through the sevens in this deck.

8	Number eight {8} offers the energy of infinity and eternal life. Black Cat, Horse, Snake, and Bee are the mediators of both worlds and advocate for closing the loop of consciousness. With eight representing the movement from one state to the other, we see how sacred animals of our homeland take us from one reality to the other, by accompanying the traveler in transition between the two.
9	Number nine {9} symbolizes wisdom and maturity. It is a clear sign that the current cycle is nearing completion, but you have a few more final touches before it is complete, much like putting the bow on a wrapped gift. We decided to represent nines through celebratory symbols of the corresponding holidays. These traditional symbols have endured over time, carrying wisdom of the ancients and reminding us that there is more to do.
10	Number ten {10} tells us that manifestation is undeniable, as we come full circle. The phrase "What goes around, comes around" helps us understand the intent of the tens. With open hearts, our ancestors celebrated life on the basis of Svarog's Circle—a folk calendar that goes back thousands of years; it was based on astronomical data, and the main holidays were determined by the position of the sun. With the changing of seasons, our world cycles through the wheel of life, manifesting all we want and need.
Ace	For each of the four periods of the solar annual cycle, there exists a divine patron with a name corresponding to its manifestation. In classic Tarot, the Ace represents the original force of the elements. In this deck, we use these gods as the embodiment of each element: Air, Water, Fire, and Fire.

HOW TO DO READINGS

Before you start your reading (regardless if it is for you or for someone else), connect with your power center. If you have ever heard the phrase "Go with your gut" or "gut instinct" you will have an idea of where to focus. In shamanism, the seat of intuition is a physical and energetic space, 2 inches below your belly button. Focus and ask for divine guidance and support. Try the words "I ask my higher self to lower my ego to less than 3%, so I may be a clear channel of the wisdom to bring the highest good of all involved." For more guidance on how to conduct a reading, please visit my website www.taniaandrushko.com for a free short tutorial.

There is plenty of information on various Tarot spreads. I would like to share my favorite ones. You may adapt each to your style, and always remember that you are your own teacher and master. This book is only a resource to share what has been most powerful in my experience.

Remember, the magic does not come from the card spread you choose; it comes from your pure intention.

CELTIC CROSS SPREAD

The Celtic Cross spread works best when you are looking for a deep understanding of all energies that are involved in the situation. This vast and all-inclusive pattern will reveal the law of cause and effect (past {5} and future {6}), which helps the reader understand how hopes and fears might influence our ability to move forward.

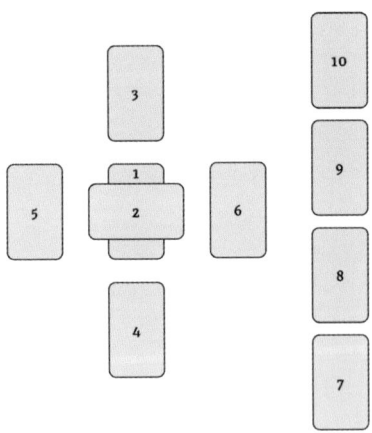

LEGEND:
1. Querent/Significator
2. Obstacle/Challenge
3. Influences/Conscious
4. Root/Subconscious
5. Past
6. Near Future
7. Suggested Approach
8. Environment
9. Hopes & Fears
10. Potential Outcome

THREE-CARD SPREAD

This is my favorite intuitive approach to reading when I am looking for a clear sign, without ambiguity. Remember that our inner knowing is never loud. In fact, it whispers the truth. Sometimes all we need is to become silent and "hear" the message from a different place, in order to recognize it. The three-card spread will silence the mind and focus on what is important and vital for the current situation.

LEGEND:
1. Past
2. Present
3. Future

1. Situation
2. Obstacle
3. Advice

1. Mind
2. Body
3. Spirit

Medicine Wheel Spread

This one is fully guided by your higher self or soul family. You may be apprehensive, but I promise that you will be pleasantly surprised once you let go of "how things should be" and allow the magic to happen. You pull the cards as per the directions of the medicine wheel (north, south, east, west, and finally the center card, which represents the Void). This is your medicine wheel, and you shall seek the messages as a breadcrumb trail to what needs to be revealed for you at this time in your life. This speaks to your mind, heart, passion, and body. The void in the middle speaks to your ultimate power to create and move forward.

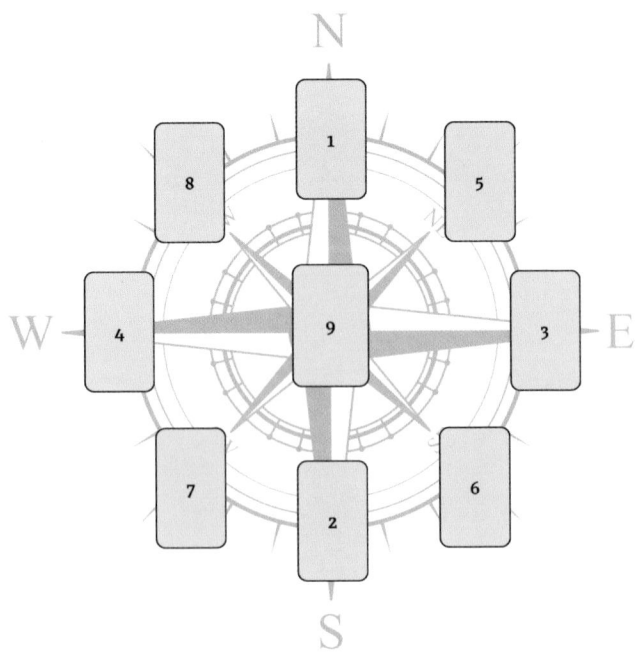

LEGEND:
1. North—Root, where the seed is planted
2. South—Creation, what is about to be birthed
3. East—Support, where to look for help/guidance
4. West—Healing, what needs to be restored
5. NE—Endings, what cords should be cut
6. SE—Shadow, what needs to be unearthed and acknowledged
7. SW—Dream, what are your highest aspirations
8. NW—Release, what is ready to be let go
9. Center—Power, the place of highest potential

MAJOR ARCANA

0—Fool

Feeling: Folly, enthusiasm, euphoria. Believing and dreaming, reality and fiction.

Ask yourself: How can my dreams become my reality? How can I find my path if my heart is full of fear?

Action: Take a Leap of Faith. Proceed with your dream and trust that when your intentions are pure and your heart is innocent, the whole universe has your back.

Essence: Knowledge applied through experience becomes wisdom.

Notes

At the stroke of midnight on the night of Ivana Kupala,[1] all of nature comes alive. Plants unroot to sing and dance with the animals to the songs of the wind and streams, and the healing powers of nature become more tangible than ever.

On that very special night, the enchanting blossom of the magic fern awakens for a brief moment. This magical, fiery flower of happiness opens on the fern in brilliant splendor, inviting everyone to seek her out in the forest.

It is said that anyone fortunate enough to pluck the flower as she awakens will be endowed with the remembrance of ancestral wisdom and the ability to hear the heartbeat of the soul of the universe. They will then understand the language of all creatures, be able to discover hidden treasures, and have authority to enter any temple. Most importantly, they will be able to find true love and happiness should they arrive with an innocence of pure intention and heart. Legend speaks of one such adventurer who had sought out the magic flower.

Long ago, one young man promised to find this flower and bestow it to his maiden. On the night of Ivana Kupala, he discovered the bloom and was lucky enough to pluck the flower at the right moment. However, hearing the cry of a small child, he turned and was alarmed to see all of hell unmasked. He tried to flee, but he was petrified since his feet were cemented to the ground. No one ever saw him again. Rumors spread. Some believed that he had been destroyed by evil spirits. Others believed that he had been killed by wild animals. Ever since, no other brave adventurer has dared to seek out the rare treasure again.

As a new dawn arrives the next morning, shadows fade away as peace and tranquility are restored to the forest by the forces of light. For the fern that was not discovered, she meekly withdraws her beautiful petals, waiting for another full year before she awakens again for a momentary breath at midsummer, inviting any hopeful adventurer to find her and be infused with her many blessings.

---

1. Night of Ivana Kupala—10 of Fire

1—Magician

Feeling: Power, magic, manifestation, inner knowing, honor.

Ask yourself: How can I align with my true purpose so I can manifest my desires for the highest good?

Action: Be open and practice self-awareness for your spiritual practices, so you can become a clear channel of your own magic.

Essence: When we practice manifestation with a pure and open heart, our higher thoughts form our reality.

Notes

In ancient times, there were special magicians who had settled on the farthest outskirts of villages in the Carpathian Mountains. They were enlightened and very soft-spoken people who were trusted guides and faithful friends with gentle hearts. Many referred to them as soothsayers, sorcerers, wizards, fortune-tellers, and charmers. In the Hutsul culture,[1] these magicians endowed with supernatural abilities were called Molfar.

Anyone who comes upon a Molfar is amazed by his power, since he is able to control the elements of nature and weather conditions, fight against demons and dark forces, predict future and fatal events, and heal the most- serious diseases. At the same time, people are touched by his gentle spirit, deep sense of spirituality, and selfless humility.

God blessed Molfar with an innate ability to see and experience the universe in a very special way. They absorb their energy directly from Mother Earth, which grants them a perfect knowledge and understanding of humanity. As guardians and protectors of this world, they are always using their special powers to selflessly honor and serve the world by working against dark forces everywhere.

Molfars work against dark spirits by manifesting positive thoughts and good intentions into reality. Being blessed with excellent communication skills, they begin by meticulously selecting the exact words necessary to represent their purpose, which are then pronounced with precise and clear articulation. The intention comes from the bottom of their heart, and it rides upon these spoken words into the four corners of this world as north, south, east, and west. These good deeds then create a powerful force into the four primary elements of our world as water, fire, air, and earth, thereby creating a ripple that attracts virtue, morality, and additional goodness to overcome the darkness.

Molfar does not journey through this purposeful life alone. He moves through this world typically with a black cat[2] that acts as a conductor of cosmic energy, a talisman, and a companion.

Molfar is the epitome of living in harmony with nature, acting in accordance with one's conscience and always seeking higher knowledge to better know oneself. It is a path of honor and altruism in the interests of serving nature and its people over and above oneself. Integrity and humility are of utmost importance so that the transformation of desires into reality remains forever pure.

---

1. Hutsul culture is a Ukrainian ethnographic group that lives in the Carpathian Mountains and has absolute connection to mother nature and spirit.
2. Black cat—8 of Air

2—High Priestess

Feeling: "I am light and love. I provide safety and protection." Quiet magic, connection, illumination, tenacity.

Ask yourself: How do I deal with obstacles and keep my heart pure and full of love?

Action: Trust your intuition. Your heart knows all the answers. Stop and listen to the whispers.

Essence: When we are united with kindness and love, there is ease in preserving connection to all of life.

Notes

In every ray of light that is cast upon all of nature, there is the spirit of a feminine goddess that is ephemeral, but always present. As a spirit embodying nature, she is mysterious, magical, divine, and infinite. She is the goddess of kindness that is ever watching over our hearth, our family, and all of our possessions. She is Beregynia, the High Priestess and the guardian of all of nature.

Beregynia moves through the world with a purpose to watch over those who live in accordance with the laws of nature. She brings the flame of fire to the family and helps preserve it from burning out, thereby ensuring that a light is always cast in the home and in the family's hearts. She teaches each family to similarly cherish and watch over the flame. Women understand that caring for the flame's warmth strengthens her love, peace, and abundance, and the brilliance of her light ignites and inspires others.

On the holiday of Beregynia, a celebration in Ukrainian villages, women go out early in the morning to the field and spread вишитий рушник[1] on the grass. They will then wash their faces with these cloths, since it is well known that the morning dew has tremendous healing properties, thus embodying the magic. The вишитий рушник can also restore vitality by providing health, strength, and longevity. They are then hung to dry on willow trees,[2] where the winds will take away and clear the negative energies from the person and restore it with healing energies.

Beregynia reminds us all to live a life of honor, respect, and protection for all living things in nature. Her radiance shines to light up not only our physical world, but also our hearts, reminding us that we are all connected in nature through the thread of love and light.

Of all of the charms, the Мотанка[3] is considered to be the strongest of all, with the spirit of Beregynia within and imparting the wisdom of ancient traditions from generation to generation. Made of a single piece of luminous pure fabric without a single seam, the charm helps the keeper of the hearth protect the home from any wrongdoers.

---

1. вишитий рушник: Embroidered cloth.
2. Willow tree—6 of Water
3. Мотанка: Traditional charm doll with the essence of Beregynia representing the purity and strength of the feminine spirit.

3—Empress

Feeling: Mother, fertility, birth, creation, action, harvesting, initiative, fruitfulness.

Ask yourself: What is being called to be birthed through me at this moment?

Action: Tap into your feminine power of creation and bring to life that which is pure, rich, and expansive.

Essence: Harmonious and aligned creation comes through the seeds that are planted with universal love.

NOTES

In the beginning, there was only the blue sea, which stretched farther than the eye could see, and on it grew a green sycamore tree—the Tree of Life.[1] When the world was just being formed, there was no sky or earth. The Tree of Life gave the world Lada, the goddess of world harmony. This goddess of the universe, beauty, and love became the Mother of All Things.

Adorned with the finest jewels and decorated in colorful clothes that are purified by heavenly fire, Lada appears to us in her dazzling beauty.

Arriving into this world on a magical chariot drawn by a pair of doves and a pair of swans, she ignites the fire of heavenly thunderstorms, drives away evil forces, and brings out the bright sun from the dark clouds.

The Mother of the Gods is married to Svarog[2] and is also recognized as the goddess of the Divine marriage and the Patroness of Childbirth and Fertility.

Coming to people on a rainbow with a baby, she holds a red apple with a vine in her hand. The baby symbolizes the world incarnate, and the apple represents the beginning of everything, the seed.

Lada brought living water to the world, and at the same time, she is there in times of death. She collects the souls of the righteous, who become the sparks of the heavens. Mother Lada then brings these souls to the human world, placing them in the wombs of women who long for a child.

Before anything else existed, the Tree of Life gave us Lada—the origin of love infused into our creation and existence. Today, the beautiful days of May and early June are dedicated to the celebration of Lada, marked by cheerful festivals. It is a time of reflection to remember that everything is birthed through her as an embodiment of feminine charm, beauty, and unconditional universal love.

---

1. Tree of Life—Major Arcana #21
2. Svarog—Major Arcana #4

4—Emperor

Feeling: Father, stability, power, aid, protection, boss.

Ask yourself: How can I use my masculine energy to lay out the foundation to be able to provide the support to myself, my family, and the collective?

Action: Create discipline and boundaries; work with authority and institutions (banks, government, schools).

Essence: When we hold the masculine energy to create order and structure, we gently direct these pillars into the flow of life.

Notes

From the fiery storm of chaos, Svarog emerges like lava from an explosive volcano. Despite his powerful stature and visage, this great ruler has a softness that conveys loving care and protection. He is the divine masculine, and he brings strength and protection to humanity.

Svarog is Lada's[1] husband and her opposite. His masculine presence brings harmony and balance to the universe. He is the male embodiment of Rod, God-Creator, god of the sky and stars, the basis of wisdom and holiness. Svarog is seen as the ruler of the world and of all deities.

Svarog is the father of all gods; he is the heavenly fire who threw the blacksmith's tongs from the sky to the ground, giving humans the ability to forge iron. From the beginning of the creation of the universe, Svarog has wielded the power to control the elements and thus forged the twelve cosmic nights (12,000 years), the sun, the moon, the evening, and the morning dawn. Svarog is the archetypal male and the embodiment of the ideal father figure, kind and strong.

Svarog has brought many gifts to the Ukrainian people. According to ancient folklore, he taught people to produce copper and iron, to build houses and forges, and to work with metal and stone alike. It was he who forged the first plow and the first gold wedding ring. Svarog built the first house and created the first millstones. He taught people to grind grain and produce flour. According to legend, he went from village to village, from house to house, teaching people a variety of useful skills for the economy and good of the community.

The wise and commanding Svarog does not wait for permission to make a difference in the lives of others. He reminds us to act with conviction and care. There is no power strong enough to limit the flow of energy toward peace and order. Trust that your actions, if taken with love in your heart, will create positive change for you and your loved ones.

---

1. Lada—Major Arcana #3

5—Hierophant

Feeling: Peaceful power, shamanism, healthy divine feminine, deep-rooted connection with ancestors, magic.

Ask yourself: How do I honor the blood in me that carries the wisdom and healing powers from my mother, grandmother, and all generations from this lifetime and all lifetimes?

Action: Look into your ancestry and seek wisdom from the lineage. Look for and find a teacher/healer who will help you evolve and unlock your powers.

Essence: When we remember who we are and where we came from, we invoke the ancestral connection within us to heal ourselves and others.

Notes

Warmth shines from the very being of the Ukrainian healer, as she busies herself in her airy cottage. Her apothecary is filled with plant medicine, which she lovingly blends with the power of the spiritual realms. The gentle healer is the embodiment of the power of love, which coincidentally is the most powerful ingredient in her arsenal. While this wise and beautiful crone has the power to wield grand spells, her knowing eyes can see what is required for the highest good.

The Hierophant is one who reveals the sacred mysteries. She is a healer and a shaman. Drawing from the ancient skills of her ancestors, she can come to know the past, present, and future. She can interpret dreams about life and death, warn against evil people, and ward off misfortune. These are powerful women who know God's will and know how to speak in God's way. Any timely and good word spoken by the healer must come true. For her, the simplest word, spoken with the power of God, possesses the power to heal any person.

Although she is well known to treat ailments with plant medicine, the healer's most common function is extraction. Healers do not exercise evil forces, nor do they engage in confrontation with any mythical creatures. Yet, when you need help to remove the foreign entity from your body, mind, or soul, the healer will forcefully and fearlessly fight against them, using prayers and orders that are fulfilled only at a precise time. Her power rests in her love, knowledge, and desire to do good in the world.

The healer brings a message of intuition and spirituality. She reminds us that there is power in the abundance of nature and the quietness of our soul. With God's guidance, you have the power to rise into the grandest version of you.

6—LOVE

Feeling: Pure heart connection; oneness; unconditional, eternal, loyal infinite love.

Ask yourself: How long will I choose to stay guarded in your castle?

Action: Take your walls down and allow unconditional love to move through you.

Essence: When we soften our hearts and are open for miracles, we unlock the potential to unite our soul's deepest connection to another.

NOTES

Кохáння[1] is a quality of love that is simple and much grander than words allow. This manifestation of love is the joining of two hearts, the deep longing, and the eternal embrace. There is nothing purer or more passionate than the commitment of love without expectation. Кохáння is a love between soulmates, defined by deep connection, trust, and loyalty. It is a gift bestowed once in a lifetime, with the truest of intentions.

Sometimes it seems that so much has been written about love that there is nothing left to write. After all, everything has already been said, in thousands of lines, words, poems, and songs. However, when true love comes to you, you instantly realize that this quality of love is especially for you. At this time, you understand that everyone has their own, special, and unique Кохáння. It is more than love. It is the energy that drives life. Кохáння is the foundation of the world and the basis for Ukrainian families. In our tradition, Кохáння is seen as a swan, the symbol of boundless love and unbreakable loyalty, because it is well known that a pair of swans remain faithful throughout life. According to our ancestors, swans, by God's will, possess the secret of eternal love, which grants lovers spiritual immortality for their loyalty and sacrifice. The swans sing, telling us how to achieve eternal love, through wholehearted commitment and loyalty to one's mate.

Love is patient and kind. Love is fiery and frantic. Кохáння is boundless and eternal. Кохáння bears all things. It allows us to be brave in knowing that this soulful relationship exists and is essential.

---

[1]. Кохáння is a feeling of deep heartfelt affection, covering a range of strong and positive emotional and mental states, from the highest virtue to deep interpersonal tenderness.

7—Chariot

Feeling: Victory, triumph, focus, bravery, success, supernatural.

Ask yourself: How do I harness my will and practice the stillness of my mind so I can be the person I want to be?

Action: Focus on what you want to achieve, and practice to unleash the potential you have in you.

Essence: Through discipline and commitment, the purification of heart can take place and enlightenment is gained.

Notes

The mystery and magic surrounding the Kharaktérnyk can be seen and felt, since he communes with nature and walks with his spirit animals. He is more than a warrior; he possesses secret knowledge and supernatural power.

At the heart of the term "kharaktérnyk" is the word "kharacter," which means "a sense of firmness and willpower." The Kharaktérnyk is a distinguished Cossack[1] warrior, who has mastered his spirit and owns his personal will. Through his magic, he can influence the will of other people.

Kharaktérnyk were once elite members of the army and were considered the army's special forces, knights of the land, and guardians of Ukraine. They were respected and feared in legends and mystical stories. People say that one Kharaktérnyk could fight against hundreds and win the battle.

These warriors were prepared from childhood. Once selected, the gifted boy became a "maid" or pupil of an older Kharaktérnyk, learning the wisdom of ancient knowledge. Over several years, the Kharaktérnyk master passed on to his young student the knowledge that he himself had been taught. This instruction was a system of psychophysical training, which included magical rituals as well as mandatory training in military craft and art. They then could shape-shift into animals, pass through walls, and travel in time.

The Kharaktérnyk conveys the message of the magnificent potential available to those who harness their internal focus and will. Enlightenment comes when the mind is still, the body is strong, and the heart is pure.

---

1. Cossack—Major Arcana #8

8—Strength

Feeling: Power, energy, action and courage, magnanimity.

Ask yourself: How can I pull my resilience and strength and gently proceed in what I want to achieve?

Action: Be courageous! Use your inner strength and fortitude as your allies in moving forward.

Essence: When our hearts are pure and brave, we can move mountains and overcome any obstacle. The intention must be for the greatest good of all involved.

NOTES

Flanked by his trusted steed, the Cossack stands strong and proud, ready to defend freedom of his people and country. His horse was considered his partner in battle and his brother for life. Like his horse, the Cossack's size and stature are the embodiment of healthy masculine energy, punctuated by the sword he holds at his chest, as both a symbol and a warning, to say, "Do not cross me. I take a stand for my people." The red coat represents the Cossack's blood running in his veins, for freedom and his country. His soft eyes belie his courage and fearsome power and remind us of his intelligence and chivalry.

One of the indispensable attributes of a Cossack was his chupryna[1] and prominent mustache, which our brave warriors inherited from their pagan ancestors. This appearance was considered divine, a symbol of chivalry and nobility, belonging to a special caste. Indeed, the Cossacks believed that if they died in the war, an angel would carry them to heaven by their hair.

His cunning skills in the battle for freedom and democracy can be summed up with the common phrase "A Zaporizhian Cossack can fool the devil himself." The Cossacks used not only military weapons, but also secret knowledge, shared from their spiritually guided caste called Kharaktérnyk,[2] who had magical abilities. Cossacks were able to withstand wars and became the force that over the centuries stood guard over the freedom and dignity of Ukraine as an independent, sovereign state.

What is surprising is that the Cossack was afraid of no one, except for a beautiful woman who might steal his heart. His heart belonged to Ukraine, and according to legends, the woman takes all the strength, courage, and magical protection from a Cossack. That is why, when joining the ranks of the Cossack brotherhood, the Zaporizhia symbolically married, because "the only bride and wife of a Cossack is freedom."

The Cossack personifies strength, courage, and indomitable will, tempered with intelligence and purity of heart. There is no halfway for the Cossack. He reminds us to commit fully and be strong.

---

1. Chupryna is a style of haircut that features a long lock of hair left on the otherwise completely shaved head.
2. Kharaktérnyk—Major Arcana #7

9—Hermit

Feeling: Soul-searching, feeling trapped, unmotivated, frustrated, feeling hopeless, powerless.

Ask yourself: How do I support myself through phases of challenge in my life?

Action: Wait. This is not a time to act. Step back.

Essence: When we disconnect from the busyness of life and go within, we honor the connection with our heart and soul, thus providing clarity in our next steps.

Notes

The soul is the inner essence of a person. She is eternal and immortal, the guide and inner knowing for all aspects of our life. According to the teachings of the ancient Ukrainian magicians, the soul is contained in the being of a person. Our ancestors cherished the sacred bond between mind, body, and soul. They would say that our soul is trapped in our body for the purpose of having the experience of being human, so we may learn lessons and evolve as spiritual beings.

The legend of Lake Synevyr tells of a rich Князь[1] who lived in a wild mountainous area where his subjects worked. The Князь's wife died early, leaving behind an only daughter with eyes so blue that the girl was named Syn. The daughter grew up to be a captivating beauty. One day, he decided to bring her into the forest. While Князь was talking with the woodcutters, Syn decided to take a walk. Enraptured by the beautiful sound of melodious music played by a lowly shepherd, Vyr, she found her way deep into a clearing in the forest. Vyr was entranced by Syn's beauty and eyes as blue as the spring sky. The young people fell instantly in love and could not imagine further life without each other.

The stern and protective Князь found out about the love between his daughter and the shepherd. Outraged, he ordered the young man to be killed. The Князь's servants dropped a large stone on Vyr, and Syn raced to the place where her beloved died. She stood on the rock and wept inconsolably, her tears making puddles and then ponds. The tears of her mournful blue eyes eventually formed the blue water of Lake Syn-e-Vyr, and the stone still remains as a solitary island. Lake Synevyr serves as a reminder of love that is as deep and pure as her blue waters.

Despite the legend and the physical reminder of Lake Synevyr, we sometimes separate ourselves from unconditional love and guidance from Spirit. It breaks the connection between our conscious and unconscious world. Then, the light of the spirit fades, leaving our soul in a state of despair. The soul always reminds us to look within to find the beauty of eternal love.

---

1. Князь is a historical Slavic title, used both as a royal and noble title, and is usually translated into English as prince or duke.

10—Fortune's Wheel

Feeling: Good luck, fate, protection, trusting that the universe has your back.

Ask yourself: What rites and practices do I participate in daily to be an intentional creator of my life?

Action: Commit to engaging in your future by weaving intentions in all that you do.

Essence: When we are conscious about what we do and what we weave, the energy we are involved in will manifest our fate and reality.

NOTES

Fortune's Wheel has the power to transmute chaos into order, confusion into clarity. Depicted in the image is the divine goddess Mokosha,[1] engaged in her sacred work of Прядіння or spinning. Because her actions are so pure and purposeful, she has the very capacity to participate in the creation of the universe. From the powerful and enchanted fleece, Mokosha spins the thread of life, fine and strong. The magic of her work draws all good things into the shining cords that flow from the wheel, affecting the futures of those whose lives are bestowed with the fruits of her craft.

The process of spinning has a double meaning that is both practical and symbolic. The thread is associated with life, which flows and breaks, intertwines generations, and weaves a cosmic fabric into matter. Ukrainians consider the gift of Mokosha—the ability to spin, weave, and embroider—to be sacred knowledge that was passed down through the maternal line. The behavior and character of a woman are reflected in the creation of her hands. The quality of the cloth depended on the purity, piety, and righteous life of the weaver. There is a Ukrainian saying, "As the spinning wheel, so the cloth will lie." If the woman was not creating from a space of high intention, the thread would be knotted and the design flawed.

Rope, lace, or thread plays a special role in our culture, and our ancestors gave them a magical meaning. In fairy tales, spun threads of hemp, flax, or wool belong to enchanted objects. The healer[2] gave the hero a magic ball of thread that showed him the path of life and protected him from dangers. The thread was used in folk medicine and was worn as a talisman. The love and intention of Mokosha are so powerful that it creates only a thread free of knots and tangles and manifests only good fate.

The Fortune's Wheel spins a future filled with serendipity. It reminds us to be conscious in our daily practices, celebrate the good days, and honor the rare days of sorrow. The energy we put into our actions will manifest our fate. With love in our hearts, look to the future and step through the door of fate, without fear.

---

1. Goddess Mokosha—Ace of Earth
2. Healer—Major Arcana #5

11—Justice

Feeling: Equity, justice, balance, honesty, morality, responsibility, diligence, karma.

Ask yourself: Am I living my life from a place of courage and honor?

Action: Choose honesty and morality to be the pillars in making decisions, then proceed with integrity.

Essence: When we live on the basis of the law of cause and effect, we become powerful, mindful manifesters of our life.

Notes

The quill is poised, hovering above the parchment, to sign a document of the highest esteem. Гетьман[1] Pylyp Orlyk is steely eyed and determined as he holds the most powerful weapon, that of written democratic law and justice among the people. The magic of this document is clear, since only someone of pure heart can wield these tools with the power of the collective.

The Constitution of Pylyp Orlyk is the first constitution that named Ukraine as a sovereign state and a part of the West, rather than belonging to the "Russian world." It is the constitution of the whole of Ukraine, bearing the principles of the independence of the Ukrainian state.

The importance of this document is not only that it was the first of its kind, but that it outlined democratic laws and rights, far ahead of its time. The innovation of Orlyk's democracy was in the division of the government into branches of power—executive, legislative, and judicial—with delegation of rights to each branch. The hetman's rights became limited under this new law, so he could not be guided by the principle "As I want, so I command." Orlyk's constitution is one of the anchors of Ukrainian identity. For Ukrainians of the twenty-first century, this document is a historical signpost because it contains many provisions that are relevant to this day.

Justice is a force that reciprocates the energy it receives. Orlyk's constitution was one of high noble intentions, giving his people the power to choose their path to success and happiness. Justice forever frames our lives around honesty, morality, rationality, and rigor. This card reminds us that we all hold power within us, and we're always meant to be fully sovereign.

---

1. Гетьман translates as hetman and stands for the highest military officer in the hetmanates area of Ukraine, the Zaporizhian Host.

12—Hanged Man

Feeling: Giving something up, detaching from injustice, surrender state.

Ask yourself: Do I trust in the timing of events or do I push back, thinking I know better?

Action: Relinquish control and step back. Wait for a better time to proceed; let go of your vision of how things should be.

Essence: When we learn to accept what is, only then are we free to move with peace in all situations. There is a divine order in everything, and our job is to trust.

Notes

As his aged hands strum lightly and his blind eyes look inward for the words and stanzas of his song, the old Kobzar sits with his kobza.[1] The stormy skies are reminiscent of dark times facing Kobzar, but the blooming flowers in the field offer a message of hope and quiet surrender.

We lovingly call kobza's singers the Kobzar, who are the people's national "Homers of Ukraine." These talented blind musicians, accompanied by young boys, traveled through the cities and villages of Ukraine, praising the brave Cossacks and their legendary pursuits. The repertoire of the Kobzars was extremely wide and colorful. They sang and played to entertain, but more importantly, to inspire a spark of patriotism for Ukraine and a love of freedom. It is not surprising that the bearers of the Ukrainian folk epics were loved and respected by the people and became a wedge in the throat of the people's oppressive authorities. The authorities finally decided to curb the freedom-loving Ukrainian kobzarstvo at any cost.

In 1930, a congress of folk singers was held in the Kharkiv Opera House, where 337 delegates from various regions of Soviet Ukraine were brought. It was explained to Kobzars that the issue of their active involvement in socialist construction caused a departure from performance traditions, and that the determination of new ideological priorities would be resolved. In fact, the convention as such did not take place. Kobzars and their underage handlers were loaded into the echelon and taken to the outskirts of Kharkiv region. There, in the forest strip, they were shot, their bodies were thrown into trenches, and their instruments were burned. While it is futile to look for some mention of this terrible tragedy in the Soviet press, the facts of the events of that time were duly recorded and shared from the mouths of living witnesses.

The kobzar is like the Hanged Man, a symbol of injustice and distrust. While difficulty surrounds him, he is content in his surrender to the flow of life and even death. Divine order cannot be avoided. Release and trust.

---

1. Kobza—3 of Earth

13—Death

Feeling: The inevitable end, death, nightmares, illness. Transition to another life.

Ask yourself: What am I ready to let go of? What has to come to an end?

Action: Embrace the transformation. Accept the inevitable. Be gentle to yourself and others.

Essence: When we open the path of least resistance, we give our soul time and space to transform, bringing in new opportunities to arise.

NOTES

Cool and distant, Marena is the Dark Mother, the patroness of the Lower World. Her beauty and allure invite us to enjoy the worldly gifts of Earth, knowing that our time here is finite. Her flowing, white locks and green eyes shine under a crescent moon, much like the glimmering sickle in her grasp, which she uses to cut the cords of life.

Marena's message is one of truth and neutrality, reminding us to live in the present and to have gratitude for life's experiences, gifts, and joys, since they will one day come to an end. She tests our strength of will to resist the base experiences, in favor of righteousness. Like the serpent, Marena can ascend to the upper limbs of the Tree of Life and descend deep beyond its roots, into the Underworld. She understands and appreciates the continuity of life and afterlife. She is content in her role in holding the infinite nature of the human soul. Marena represents the female manifestation of the dark side of being and the subconscious of our universe.

According to Old Slavic legends, the goddess Marena heard of the birth of the sun from Kolyada,[1] the goddess of Sky, to bring hope and joy to the world. She searched for Kolyada in an effort to halt the birth but failed and descended into the afterworld. To this day, Marena emerges every winter, freezing the earth, sowing discord, and causing disease and hunger. In folklore, Marena was the antithesis of Kupala,[2] and her gift is the contrast of light to dark. She is a winter deity whose stories were used to scare naughty children into appropriate behavior and whose legend elicits deep respect for life and death.

Marena reminds us to live in the moment, drinking in all aspects of the experience, knowing that joy expands and difficulty instructs. There is no need to fear her, but be mindful and cherish all of life's gifts. Marena teaches us of the neutrality of all events, including death. Her presence helps us remain vigilant in our decisions and surrender to life's lessons with grace and gratitude.

---

1. Kolyada—Ace of Air
2. Kupala—Ace of Fire

14—Temperance

Feeling: Waiting, sadness, sorrow, annoyance, frustration, irritation.

Ask yourself: How can I surrender to what is and let go of my expectations of how I want it to be?

Action: Focus on what you can influence and control—your thoughts, beliefs, and actions.

Essence: When we trust in divine timing and focus on being, we are gifted with peace and the power of presence.

Notes

The dappled sky sparkles in the morning mist as we gaze toward our dreams and wishes. The path of temperance is inviting, but not always clear. Lit only with muted sunshine, this foggy trail is the only access point to what we desire. Trees and foliage line the footpath, and the sturdy well offers the wanderer life-sustaining water along their journey. Take heart and walk on, for you have all you need, and be assured that soon the fog will lift.

The well is not only a household source of water, but also a public domain, cared for by residents of small Ukrainian villages. These wells were created for the common good of the village and were protected, nurtured, ennobled, and cleaned by those who lived nearby. Digging wells was considered a primary and honorable task for all residents of the village. This was both a place of functionality and of gathering for the community.

It was the well that created an energetic space to connect and to share news. A traveler could quench his thirst and rest here. Young people gathered near the wells for holidays, led dances, and declared their love. While watering their horses, Cossacks met and said goodbye to their sweethearts. The songs of the Kobzars about the past of the Ukrainian people were heard here. People came to the well in days of good luck and bitter disappointments.

A beautiful legend tells a story about an old grandmother who lived in the Carpathian Mountain. She was teaching her young and impatient granddaughter a lesson of temperance. She asked the granddaughter to bring the bucket of water from the well. The young granddaughter wanted to finish her house chores quickly, so she hurried, losing water along the way. The wise grandmother would not accept the partially filled bucket and sent her back to refill it. The frustration was rising in the young child. This living lesson went on for years, before the granddaughter realized that temperance is the key. When she finally brought presence into her work and stopped rushing to get it done, she actually started to enjoy the task of fetching water. When the excited granddaughter finally went to share her enlightenment, her beloved had died. The wise woman had gone to another realm, since she served her purpose in this lifetime.

While we may wish to rush toward our desires, we often miss the beauty of the journey that comes with patience and presence. When we surrender to the task and embark on all things with love, we are blessed with the gift of being. Trust that this path is the right and perfect one for you.

15—Witch

Feeling: Evil, violence, severance, misfortune, hardship, jealousy, anger.

Ask yourself: What practices do I keep to protect myself and my life from negative situations?

Action: Introduce rituals to your routine so no one and nothing can interfere with your inner peace, purity of soul, and clarity of path.

Essence: This is a warning to be careful whom I allow in my world, and an urgency to make conscious decisions around boundaries that keep me safe.

Notes

A narrow beam of light plays off the Witch's face while she is shrouded in darkness and gloom. Her natural beauty conceals the power that lies within, waiting for the perfect moment to cast her evil spells. Her black, unkempt hair bears the raven's feathers and is crowned with barren twigs and poisonous berries. The Witch is youthful and alluring, since she draws on the energy of the natural world, but the darkness within her cannot be disguised.

The nature of the Witch is twofold. On the one hand, she belongs to the world of demons and the afterlife. On the other hand, she lives on Earth and belongs to the world of people. A Witch is a woman endowed with extraordinary demonic abilities to harm people. This woman knows evil spirits, possesses supernatural power, and uses it to bring harm and manipulation. She can shape-shift and be transformed into whatever suits her means. A frog, a snake, a wheel from a cart, a cloth, or a ball of thread; there is no knowing until her evil will is done. She embodies duality in her appearance. During the day she is a very pretty young girl or woman with a passionate appeal; at night, a scruffy old hag.

Every year, during the night of Ivana Kupala,[1] all the Witches become young and beautiful and flock to the most famous coven, which is on Лиса Гора[2] near Kyiv. In these playgrounds, illuminated by bonfires, witches and other evil forces take part in wild orgies and parties, after the festivities of the summer solstice. There is much drinking, dancing, and throwing swords and arrows at one another, while they start to steal souls from people and hide them in jars. This bedlam continues until the rooster crows, welcoming the new day and new light, sending the Witches home to their hovels and covens.

The Witch may look stunning at first glance, but take caution: she brings evil and hardship. Even if she is hidden from us, Witch is near. She is cunning and manipulative, spreading negativity and ill feelings. Protection is a priority now. Purify your inner and outer surroundings to bring peace and clarity.

---

1. Night of Ivana Kupala—10 of Fire
2. Лиса Гора: Barren Mountain.

16—TOWER

Feeling: Sudden, unexpected change; epiphany; events will be happening in a speedy manner.

Ask yourself: When I feel there is no way to escape the threatening situation, do I trust that Spirit has my back?

Action: Be open and surrender. Remain present and seek the opportunity to transform what you might perceive as a negative event to experiencing growth and evolution.

Essence: When we are in distress, we do not serve ourselves or others. Life happens for me and through me.

NOTES

_____

_____

_____

_____

_____

The dark roofs and spires bring to mind the challenge that befell this stronghold, since it was witness to numerous wars and battles. The Tower is depicted as the famous defensive castle known as the Khotyn Fortress, located on the rocky shores of the Dnister River. In fact, the city of Khotyn became a war trophy to many enemies. Yet, its walls provided refuge and hope for settlers and craftsmen, ready to build a life of prosperity.

The Khotyn Fortress is placed at a crossroads, where many travelers would reach the security of its walls. The hope for a brighter future was often dashed by the frequent attacks on Khotyn. The Tower tells of unexpected changes and surprising events that, although sometimes painful, bring about positive outcomes.

The Khotyn Fortress is the so-called arena of the largest combat events and decisive military conflicts. At the beginning of the seventeenth century, the army of the Turkish sultan Osman II advanced into Ukraine and Poland to conquer Europe. Once the Khotyn Fortress was surrounded by the enemy, a sudden and unexpected event occurred. The river overflowed its banks and flooded the canyon across its width, which led the embarrassed enemy into retreat, saving the fortress and its inhabitants. This had never happened before and has never happened since but serves as proof that extraordinary and unforeseen events happen when we surrender to the mercy of Spirit.

There is a legend about "the Wet Spot" on the outer wall of the fortress that can still be seen today. The story tells of a tyrant prince who once ruled in the Khotyn Fortress. In order to strengthen his political position, he decided to promise his daughter's hand in marriage to a foreign ruler, as his bride. The girl was secretly in love with the local governor and refused to marry for her father's political gain. When the father witnessed the daughter's defiance, he ordered her to be buried alive in the fortress wall. The girl did not resist; she only cried bitterly for her lost love and life. Her heart's connection to her beloved was stronger than her fear of death. The stain, according to legend, will not dry until the lovers are reunited.

The Tower brings a message of shocking or unexpected events, which may be painful or emotional. Be open to the lessons, remain present, and surrender to what is.

17—Star

Feeling: Eternity, mystery, far far away, galaxy, dreams, new hopes, eternal infinite night.

Ask yourself: What might be keeping me away from manifesting my dreams into reality?

Action: Believe in yourself and your divine power; know that you are supported. Make a wish upon the falling star—trust that it will come true.

Essence: When dreams are keeping us awake, it's time to lean into the presence of ancestors in the night sky to help manifest miracles.

Notes

The Star lives in the darkest of skies, which is the kingdom of the ancestral spirit and supreme power. Star is youthful and innocent, with light shining from the depths of her dark eyes. Her raven locks sparkle with the reflection of celestial bodies placed there by the Creator's own hand. She is forward moving as she glances back, waiting for and inviting us to follow her light.

Filled with wanderlust and eagerness, Star has an uncanny intuition and sense of direction. She is wanting to guide us into the unknown with her healing, faith, and inspiration. Star possesses the gift of vision, drawing upon the heavens to bestow us with dreams and grant us our heartfelt wishes. She lights the path that leads us to the manifestation of our deepest desires.

According to the beliefs of our ancestors, stars were rarely given names, because they believed that they were burning candles of human's souls. As soon as someone is born, God lights a candle and places it in the sky. When a person lives harmoniously on Earth, their candle burns with a clear, pure light and signifies a long, happy life. Conversely, if a person lives a chaotic, disorderly existence, their star burns with a weak, pale fire. Each human soul is shining in the infinite galaxy, guided by Star's purity and wonder. When you see a falling star, make a wish, since that is a very special moment of the soul coming back home. Trust that your wish will be granted.

You are precious and miraculous, with the power to manifest all that you dream. Star invites you to dream big and trust in yourself.

18—Moon

Feeling: Guessing, illusion, not seeing things as they are, secrets that are hidden from you, darkness.

Ask yourself: How can I align myself to be in rhythm with the greater flow of life?

Action: Be patient and allow grace to guide you as you make time to map out the actions, plans, and projects so it is supporting your dreams.

Essence: When we rush the process, we might not have the best outcome possible, since not all the details are illuminated at the beginning.

Notes

The Moon is dark and mysterious, his beauty and magnetism utterly undeniable. His smooth face and chiseled features glow softly, in spite of the fact that he remains partially hidden. Although you may feel drawn to rush toward him and his temptations, be patient, for Moon holds more than meets the eye.

It is not surprising that the moon has historically been used as a timekeeper and calendar, marking days and seasons with his waning and waxing. Although the basis of the modern calendar is associated with the sun, the traditional lunar calendar of our ancestor circles around the archetypal triad of life-death-rebirth.

The Moon stands above the whole world. He is all seeing, all knowing, a soothsayer, and clairvoyant and is therefore always treated with respect. The new moon in the Ukrainian ancestors' picture of the world is associated with a favorable outcome for agricultural work, engagements, and weddings. It is believed that everything that starts on the new moon will end happily.

The full moon carries a much-different energy and thus invites a different focus. It is believed that the Moon, fully pictured in the sky, promotes healing practices and orders the release of what no longer serves even curses. When collecting a healing potion, herbalists still take into account the phases of the moon, focusing on the increase or decrease of its visibility and power.

The moon's magnetic pull is impossible to resist, drawing us into its dark and mysterious essence. Its serene glow unveils chiseled features, though partially shrouded in mystery. As the guardian of time, the moon whispers a celestial reminder to embrace patience. In this cosmic tapestry, allow grace to lead the way as you meticulously map out actions, plans, and projects, ensuring they align harmoniously with the symphony of your dreams.

19—Sun

Feeling: Abundance in all its forms (material, health, wealth, opulence, emotional, spiritual), warmth, source, prosperity, luck, positive energy, clarity, joy, success in business.

Ask yourself: How can I allow abundance to flow through me?

Action: Be open to bring prosperity to your life and to the lives of others. This is the time that presents the most possibilities and opportunities.

Manifestation: When we allow source to work through us, we are bringing unlimited abundance to our life.

Notes

The opulent woman depicted in this card is full of warmth and feminine energy. The richness of her clothing and adornments signifies all good things, both of this world and of the heavens. Her beauty cannot be denied, but the sun shines in spite of her onlookers, sharing her energy with all who behold her. She is both common and regal, reminding others of the importance of self-love and universal love.

The sun is a heavenly fire that illuminates all resources so we, humans, can manifest anything and everything we want. She is considered the center of the world and the source of life, often showing herself in the form of other deities. If we compare the lifetime of the sun with the age of mankind, it can be considered that the sun exists forever, giving Mother Earth its life-creating force. The sun brings to the cosmos natural order of abundance and happiness.

So loved was this energy that the Ukrainian people wished to keep her warmth and love close to themselves and their families. The circle, a symbol of the sun, infinity, and feminine love, was richly represented in Вишиванка—the Ukrainian embroidered shirt. In ancient times, the ritual of embroidery was very sacred and intimate—it was undertaken on certain days only, with pure and bright thoughts, always washing your hands before embarking upon this loving act and always putting positive energy into one's work. Women of each family created specific embroidery patterns to depict the sun on all her family's shirts, infusing love with each stitch. This traditional garment symbolizes and carries the spiritual wealth, high wisdom, and traditional connection of many generations—a connection that is not interrupted for centuries. It is passed from generation to generation, preserved as a priceless relic.

At that time, women did not copy other people's creations and did not embroider them from other products or patterns; their works were unique. The woman possessed the "language" of ornamental writing, where through colors, lines, and patterns she created a unique heirloom, coded with good fate for herself or a loved one. Sewing someone else's pattern for a shirt, for example, meant taking on someone else's fate. Embroidery was not work or science but, rather, artful magic, which conveyed one's worldview and inner energy by encoding it on canvas.

The Sun offers us trust that love and openness are the means to all abundance and happiness, for us and the world.

20—CALL

Feeling: Life review, rebirth, making a decision, change.

Ask yourself: How can I support myself in following my calling?

Action: Hear the whispers of your heart. Listen to the subtle sounds from the universe that are calling you. It is time to believe, take action, move forward.

Essence: When we follow the calling of our true purpose, we allow alignment to fully guide us.

NOTES

The trembita offers a resonant call to your soul, with its gentle but persistent tones. This traditional Alpine horn is called the "Princess of the Carpathian Mountains." The slender beauty of trembita must be experienced, since its voice is deep and full, in contrast to her long, slim body. When trumpeted from the heights of the Carpathians, its song may be heard throughout the world and far into the cosmos. It cannot be ignored.

There is a specific frequency emitted from the trembita, which lovingly wakes us from our slumber. It is said to be endowed with the voice of God because of its unique construction from the thunderwood spruce tree that is struck by a lightning bolt. Craftsmen search through distant forests for weeks looking for this tree and settle for those no younger than 120 years old. Only this perfect combination will bestow the proper energy and frequency for your soul to hear trembita's call.

In ancient times, the trembita was used as a signaling and communication instrument. The trembita would be the first clock for the inhabitants of the Carpathian Mountains, its body casting shadows like an ancient sundial. It worked with the sun's movements to cast shadows throughout the day, alerting shepherds[1] in the mountains to the time of day. Because their pitch reaches 2.5 octaves, and the sound can travel more than 10 km, the trembitas have been constant companions to the shepherds. With their help, flocks of sheep were summoned and even guests were invited to their homes. The trembita was also used to create musical messages to communicate with neighboring villages, warn about perceived threats, or simply welcome a new day! The trembita is the epitome of inventiveness, using the finest gifts from nature to bring valuable sacred tools to the people of the land.

The trembita offers not only a wake-up call, but also a persistent nudge toward creativity and innovation. Its song is the sound of the universe tirelessly whispering messages of the soul. Surrender to the song. Wake up. Listen. Believe.

---

1. Shepherd—5 of Air

21—WORLD

Feeling: Assuredness, creation, travel completion, immigration, change of place.

Ask yourself: What legacy will I leave behind once my time is up?

Action: Travel, enjoy, explore, nourish the inner voyager, and expand to new opportunities. This is the time to enjoy all experiences and celebrate life on Mother Earth.

Essence: We are a creation of unconditional love and unconditional love flows through us, in this vibrant and loving World.

NOTES

The Tree of Life grows in a tangle of intricately colored limbs and flowers, its details luminous through the decorative glass. This eternal tree blooms through all seasons, casting bright symmetrical patterns on those who pass by. With leaves, buds, and blooms growing simultaneously in the colorful window, the Tree of Life is the image of continuity and fulfillment.

The Tree of Life is the basis of our ancestors' worldview. This symbolic tree has long been seen as a kind of model of the universe, representing the order that opposes chaos and creates the emergence of all living things. It is the most sacred symbol marking the three foundations of the world: Yav is the visible and tangible world, Nav is the spiritual world of angels and ancestors, and Prav is the world of customs and ceremonies.

In all depictions, the Tree of Life blooms continually. Some flowers have already faded, leaving berries or fruit behind, some have just blossomed, while others are waiting to burst from their buds. Each of the flowers represents a different stage of human life. Ripe fruits symbolize the results of human actions and achievements. The flower is the lush and fragrant present, in which we all live. The buds represent future generations to come. The top of the World Tree is usually decorated with a special flower, called the Fire of Life, which is flanked by two light guardian spirits, usually in the form of birds. The roots of the Tree are immortal, like life itself.

According to legend, the Tree of Life grows on the living-stone Alatyr in the middle of the galaxy. With its thirst for life, it grew deep into the once-impenetrable chaos. The Creator tirelessly protected the tree, hovering over her for thousands of years, until the Tree of Life finally gave birth to divine Lada,[1] goddess of the universe, thus creating the unity of heaven and earth.

The Tree of Life brings security and groundedness to our existence, coupled with vibrant color, joy, and infinite love. There is no way to fail, so trust the security of Mother Earth and enjoy the abundant opportunities to grow.

---

1. Lada—Major Arcana #3

MINOR ARCANA
Air

8 of Air

ACE OF AIR

Feeling: New beginnings under difficult situations, truth revealed, new endeavors.

Ask yourself: How can I support myself when bringing my bright ideas to life?

Action: Use your intelligence to see the unlimited possibilities to achieve what is needed now as the first step.

Essence: When we seek wisdom from within, we find we have access to infinite consciousness.

NOTES

Bathed in radiant bright color, Kolyada appears on the shortest day of the year. She carries the Christmas Star, for all to see, spreading hope into the world. Kolyada is present in the world, but her brilliance is not of this world. Her magnificent brilliant light makes this enchanting goddess beautiful beyond belief.

Kolyada is the ancient Ukrainian goddess of the sky, mother of the sun, and wife of Dazhbog, the god of light. Her name comes from the word "kolo," which means circle and is the ancient name for the sun. On the winter solstice, the old sun dies and is resurrected in its youngest manifestation. Every year on the longest night of winter, Kolyada gives birth to a baby god named Bozhich—the new sun, the light, the new year, the son of Dazhbog.

Legend tells us that when infinite darkness came to Mother Earth, the deity Rod told Kolyada (who was almost ready to give birth to her child) to seek solitude and to bear the child alone. "Dear Kolyada," he commanded, "go to the Earth Mother, where the circle of gold breeds! Here you will find the place to give birth to Bozhich by yourself."

But Чорнобог, the Dark God, heard that the Light would be born, and sent his wife, Marena,[1] to find Kolyada and end her life, so that the sun would die and never shine on the people. Чорнобог wished to do harm to the people and believed that they would perish in the darkness from hunger and cold, without Kolyada's son. Marena frantically ran across the earth in search of Kolyada, chasing her through the forests and fields. Kolyada, heavy with child, could not run away fast enough, so she turned herself into an inconspicuous goat. Furious, Marena ran past the goat, not paying attention to the inconspicuous gray animal.

Meanwhile, Kolyada entered the reeds and gave birth to the golden-faced baby, the baby god, Bozhich. Suddenly the world changed. The cold darkness disappeared. The sun's rays covered the earth, and people fell to their knees, welcoming the birth of the Golden Sun.

Kolyada reminds us of our inner strength and potential. There are new beginnings afoot. Be resolute in your purpose, even if you are tested and challenged. Good things will come.

---

1. Marena—Major Arcana #13

Page of Air

Feeling: Curiosity, new focus, and thoughts of new beginnings. Light and purity.

Ask yourself: How do I strategically plan and map out the path that will help me create a life of purpose and meaning?

Action: Expand in curiosity; get involved in something new that gives you excitement. Be courageous, be smart, and intuitively pursue what feels right for you.

Essence: The immortality of the human soul allows us to explore infinite possibilities.

Notes

The periwinkle blooms along delicate, climbing vines, and their uniform petals turn the harshest of terrains into something beautiful. The vines wind their way through the grass, finding higher anchors upon which to bloom, reminding us all to remain curious and hopeful of how life can unfold in unexpected ways.

In Ukrainian villages, periwinkle was one of the main features of a traditional wedding, being used to weave into wreaths celebrating the new union and as a reminder of the strength and sanctity of marriage.

By the bright fire on a warm Kupala night, young women wove wreaths, listening to the song of the waves of the Cheremosh River. Legend speaks of Lada, the youngest and most beautiful of the village girls, who was enamored with picking flowers. On this night, she wandered into the forest, seeking a harvest. She found herself scared and alone. She called out to her friends in vain, but only her echo responded.

Miracles in the forest revealed themselves as unseen flowers bloomed under the darkened bushes. Their delicate petals shone silvery under the moon, beckoning Lada. She plucked a flower and wove it into her colorful wreath. It then lit up with an alluring light, and multitudes of supple green leaves appeared, with delicate, five-petaled, blue flowers appearing among them.

Lada then heard a quiet, sublime voice speak: "The five petals of this flower are the five foundations of a happily married life. The first petal is beauty, the second is tenderness, the third is infinite love, the fourth is harmony, and the fifth is loyalty. Keep them in your heart for the rest of your life."

Guided by the brilliant light, Lada found her way out of the forest, where she came upon a beautiful man standing by the river. When their eyes met, they both knew that they were kindred spirits. He asked for her beautiful wreath, and Lada humbly handed the ring of flowers to him. From that time forth, they lived a long and happy life together. To this day, young people weave periwinkle wreaths to ensure that their marriage will be filled with happiness and everlasting love.

Periwinkle is the most important symbol of life, representing new beginnings and the extraordinary potential of what is to come. Its vines, like trails on a great cosmic map, lead us to the possibility of novel and exciting experiences and relationships yet unseen.

Messenger of Air

Feeling: The embodiment of life and birth (both in the physical and spiritual realms).

Ask yourself: How can I change my mindset from one who believes that "life happens to me" to the broader truth in knowing that "life happens for me."

Action: Invite more trust into your heart and mind so that you can consider and appreciate situations from a higher perspective.

Essence: When we truly know who we are in our heart, we can trust in the universe that it will conspire to watch over and guide us.

Notes

The stork, with its grace and expansiveness, flies great lengths to reach a suitable nesting place. Traveling great distances to faraway locales in the cold seasons, the stork always returns to her native land, bringing surprising and pleasant change to the home where she nests. This beautiful bird brings a message of good fortune, joy, and a future filled with happiness and harmony.

In Ukrainian traditions, the stork is considered a symbol of the annunciation—when the angel Gabriel announced to Mary that she will bear the Christ Child. This message is closely connected with the arrival of storks in spring, which brings good news that the cold of winter is over and that summer will soon be here.

The stork is a herald of good news. Like the changing season, she encourages us to look forward to warmer times and happy announcements, knowing that we are protected and safe. It is said that the spirit of the unborn child awaits with quiet anticipation for the arrival of the stork to usher the new babe into the world. This is why young maidens believed that dreaming of storks meant that they would soon be pregnant.

In ancient times, Tatars attacked many Ukrainian villages, taking whatever they could and setting fire to the rest. Many of its inhabitants were killed, while the rest were taken into captivity. The babies, believed to be unable to survive, were thrown into the fires. The storks saw this horrific act and called upon the Cossacks[1] for help. However, help did not come quickly enough, so the storks took action immediately. They descended into the roaring fire to retrieve the children in their beaks and lifted them high above the flames, delivering them from danger. The Cossacks eventually heard the cry of a child ring out and rushed to save the children. They caught up with the horde and were able to save the villagers. Since then, the stork has become both loved and respected in Ukraine.

The stork reminds us to trust that difficult times are temporary and will soon pass.

---

1. Cossack—Major Arcana #8

Queen of Air

Feeling: High intelligence, strong self-esteem, clear communication, well organized, mentally strong.

Ask yourself: How can I best use my intellect to achieve what I desire in alignment with the highest good for all?

Action: Use your brilliance, directness, and good advice to bring more light and support for those around you.

Essence: When we work to serve our community, we understand that collectively, we create a ripple serving a higher and grander purpose for the good of all.

Notes

Remembered as the golden-haired, radiant Ukrainian Княгиня[1] from Kyiv, Anna Yaroslavna was remarkable for making Ukraine famous throughout all of Europe. Anna married King Henry I of France, representing her homeland with great honor, and she became the first recorded emigrant from Ukraine to Europe.

As a young child, Anna's father, Yaroslav the Wise, insisted that she be well educated. Under the supervision of her mother, Anna quickly mastered Latin, ancient Greek, and the basics of medicine. It was this intelligence that later wowed the French when she first arrived to their country. Upon her marrying the king, word quickly spread across the country of the incredible intellect and enchanting beauty of Anna of Kyiv, the queen of France.

Anna's keen aptitude for education allowed her to learn the French language very quickly. This allowed her to assume a significant position within French society as consort and to actively participate in governing the country with her husband. His signed decrees often included the following: "With the consent of my wife, Anna." Anna's reputation became well known, and Pope Nicholas II wrote to her directly, making her the only woman he ever corresponded with. Upon the king's passing, Anna became regent of France, leading as mother to her young son.

Anna of Kyiv's legacy was to promote the value of education in France. Anna's love and respect for formal education were extended to influence the French culture, colored with the spirit of her homeland childhood experiences. She became a catalyst in initiating Franco-Ukrainian relations, which had always been a goal of hers: to make her homeland well recognized and respected across the country of France.

Anna reminds us that though we may at times lack self-confidence and struggle to defend our own dignity, we can always stay strong and focused on the same underlying values. In knowing that we all are tied by common threads, we can use this knowledge to ensure we continue to work unselfishly in the interests of all. This work toward unified harmony will ripple into space and time as Anna's legacy spread across an entire continent.

---

1. Княгиня is a historical Slavic title, used both as a royal and noble title, and is usually translated into English as princess or duchess.

KING OF AIR

Feeling: Highly intelligent, wise, knowledgeable, and clever. Reason over instinct, creating laws, structures, and judgments.

Ask yourself: How can I take what I know to better plan with greater intention?

Action: Apply your wisdom and knowledge thoughtfully as you seek the things you desire.

Essence: When we are committed and determined to strategically realize our goals, we will also create a legacy that will surpass the bounds of space and time.

NOTES

The King of Air rules with reason and intellect, looking toward the future with brightness in his eyes and balance in his demeanor. Thanks to many reforms and achievements that had a colossal impact on the development of Kyivan Rus,[1] he was dubbed Yaroslav the Wise, an outstanding statesman and politician, Великий князь[2] of Kyivan Rus, and a famous military leader. His policy was distinguished by farsightedness and balanced decisions, and he significantly strengthened the position of the Kyivan Rus in Europe.

Being a farsighted and extremely intelligent person, he purposefully pursued very effective public and political policy throughout his life. The period of Yaroslav the Wise's reign is considered an era of greatness. It was at this time that Kyivan Rus reached the zenith of its power and became one with the most-powerful European states.

The ruler was very fond of reading and writing, and his legendary library consisted of several thousand books that are still sought after by historians and archeologists. By order of Yaroslav, the translation of numerous valuable manuscripts and books from European languages into Ukrainian commenced for the first time. He also wrote Руська Правда, the first set of judicial laws of ancient Ukraine that combined civil and criminal law and all judicial processes of that historical time.

Full of desire to strengthen the position of Kyivan Rus in Europe, Yaroslav encouraged the marriage of his children with the royal dynasties of the Old World. He, himself, married the daughter of the Norwegian king. All of his children married members of the Continent's ruling families, and his four daughters became queens of four different countries: Norway, Slovakia, France, and England. Thanks to the fact that the prince's daughters were married to European monarchs, many people who follow their genealogy are considered descendants of Yaroslav the Wise. With careful and conscious strategy in mind, this ruler improved the state of his country and his people. Due to his extensive family ties, Yaroslav was called the "Father-in-Law of Europe."

Yaroslav the Wise always practiced cautious but proactive planning for the achievement of his objectives. There was no aspiration too great for his own intelligence, focus, and proactive planning, proving that his legacy is attributed to the application of great wisdom and focused execution.

---

1. Kyivan Rus: A state in eastern and northern Europe from the late ninth to the mid-thirteenth century, with Kyiv as a capital. It is Ukraine's cultural ancestor.
2. Великий князь: Translates as grand duke.

2 OF AIR

Feeling: Duality, making a choice, thinking about options, opposites. One is riches, magnificence, fortune; on the other hand, it is suffering, death, sadness, mortification.

Ask yourself: How can I soften the heaviness of decision-making?

Action: Accept the duality of life so you can proceed lightly.

Essence: When we see love in each aspect of our life, we move gracefully.

NOTES

The beauty and tradition of a handcrafted Ukrainian Вишитий рушник[1] cannot be denied. Its delicate patterns are woven into the sturdy white fabric. The contrast of simple shapes and intricate details is symbolic of the duality of all life. The embroidered cloth's bold red and dark-black threads echo this duality, with their traditional meanings: red is love and life; black is sorrow and death. This sacred cherished Вишитий рушник is a simple reminder of contrast and opposites, dilemma and choice.

Ukrainian Вишитий рушник is an indispensable attribute of folklore and rituals. Important events in the life of the people were never without this sacred embroidered cloth. Newborns were welcomed on them, and the cloths accompanied the elders in their final passing. The important role of the Вишитий рушник in the life of the Ukrainian people involves the spheres of life and death. It is a representation of the road of life, beginning at birth, filled with important and joyful events, and ending with death, the completion of the life path.

An embroidered cloth has a special place in the history and culture of Ukraine. It was usually given by mothers or grandmothers to their daughters and sons, or from a bride to the groom. In the embroidery of the Вишитий рушник are ornaments related to the images of goodness, beauty, and protection from all evil on earth. This ornate stitching is how Ukrainian people wove their dreams into spells, through mysterious and magical symbols.

Ukrainian Вишитий рушник were created by women in almost a meditative state, when women would weave their energy into the cloth. Each time you take a red thread and start embroidering, you add all of your wishes to the person to whom this towel will belong. The black thread is a reminder of the reverence and connection of all life and the eventuality of death. There is always a beginning and an end.

---

1. Вишитий рушник: Sacred embroidered cloth.

3 OF AIR

Feeling: Sadness, grief, emotional pain, broken heart, loneliness.

Ask yourself: Do I allow things to flow freely or am I attached to outcomes and interfere with the movement of life?

Action: Release and let go. The act of liberation, or freeing yourself, is highly recommended at this time.

Essence: When we release what is not serving us any longer, we welcome new light into our mind, heart, and soul. New things can enter our reality only if we have space for them.

NOTES

As the sun sets in the pale-crimson sky, the flutist fills the air with gentle sounds from the Ukrainian flute, Sopilka. The warm wood stands out in its appearance and clarity, while autumn fields blow in the breeze. The forlorn call of this wooden flute is juxtaposed by the youth and beauty of its player, who delicately plays the instrument and shares its song. The singing of the flute is a symbol not only of the beauty of the soul, of love, but freedom and joy and testifies for the Truth.

The flute is perhaps the oldest and most widespread wind instrument in Ukraine. It first appeared within the territory of modern Ukraine 20,000 years ago, and therefore Ukraine is considered the homeland of this musical instrument. Historically, these woodwinds were crafted from the elder or viburnum tree.[1]

In legends and fairy tales, the flute hears and sees what people want to hide from one another. The flute symbolizes the truth that can no longer be hidden, which drips with tears from the branches of the viburnum, begging to be heard. There was also a belief that if you make a flute from a viburnum, a son will appear in the family.

It is believed that the flute absorbed the singing heart, the free spirit, and the cheerful disposition of our ancestors. In fairy tales, the melody of the woodwind is an image of light and truth, which will help free oneself from evil spells or recognize deception.

In Ukrainian history, flutists were shepherds[2] who, with the help of this magical instrument, were able to find peace in their hearts during times when they felt lonely or sad while away from their family in the summer months. The melody of the flute has been known to heal a broken heart and any emotional pain.

The flute song is lonely and solemn, calling us to feel and allow our feelings to move through us. So emotional is the music that we can't help but allow our heart to mourn and our eyes to shed tears. This is a good thing, since we are able to release the emotion and create space to welcome new light into our lives.

---

1. Viburnum tree—6 of Fire
2. Shepherd—5 of Air

4 OF AIR

Feeling: Loss, dishonor, vigilance, retreat, solitude, exile.

Ask yourself: How can I withstand difficult times while, at the same time, seek to move with freedom within my life?

Action: Nourish your soul and take time for healing and regrouping. Then you can tune into your inner guidance.

Essence: When we listen to our intuition with a clear and healthy mind, the answers we need are brought to light.

NOTES

The flag stands solitary and peaceful, requiring no introduction or explanation. Its bright-blue and gold bands signify strength and clarity in the pursuit of freedom and peace. The flag flies high so that all may find comfort in its presence as they journey home. During the years of restored Ukrainian independence, the national flag has become a symbol of pride, which has firmly rooted itself in our consciousness. Life without it cannot even be imagined.

The flag is a beautiful visual depiction of the endless harvest fields set against the wide-open blue skies of the Ukrainian landscape. The flag was a symbol of respect, unity, and honor of the Ukrainian people, especially through the Revolution of Dignity and the Patriotic War of Independence against Russian invaders.

With the declaration of Ukraine's independence, the flag was ordained as the national symbol of the Cossacks[1] and has endured ever since. The Ukrainian people embrace it as a symbol of their culture and traditions. Now, the flag can be seen at numerous positions on the eastern front—blue-yellow ribbons and chevrons flying high, proclaiming the heart of a nation bounded by courage, resilience, mettle, and tenacity.

Some modern researchers trace the tradition of using yellow and blue colors back to ancient times. The colors were organically woven into the Christian religion, and today in Ukrainian Orthodox churches. Fire and water are the greatest sanctities, which are expressed through yellow and blue. Many faiths look at blue as the power of Spirit, and yellow as faith.

Quiet and humble in its message, the flag is bold in presence. Every time we look upon its unfurled colors dancing in the wind, it reminds us to look for guidance within, to see that the path is already clear to us and that support in the community is nearby. It is a sacred talisman that speaks to the freedom, invincibility, and dignity of the human spirit.

---

1. Cossack—Major Arcana #8

5 OF AIR

Feeling: Needing to wait, not seeing the full picture, surrendering to the long road ahead.

Ask yourself: How do I find new alternative solutions when I feel like I've reached a dead end?

Action: Seek out innovative possibilities and approaches that are beyond your habits and patterns.

Essence: When we accept that the defeat is an illusion, we find opportunity and courage to look toward the unexpected with an open mind.

NOTES

The shepherd rests high in the luxuriant Carpathian Mountains, with only his sheep as companions. His flute soothes him and his flock, passing time with a melody of safekeeping and surrender. He is solitary and peaceful in his task of caring for his flock. This job was definitely not for the faint of heart and was reserved for a fearless, courageous, prudent, honest, and fair person. It was also a position that invited the shepherd to have a deep devotional connection not only to the flock, but also with the enveloping Mother Nature.

Shepherding or sheep breeding is a tradition that has evolved over a long period of time. Sheep are treasured in Ukraine and have been bred since ancient times, since they provided the peasants with the most-necessary products: skins, wool, meat, and milk. The craft of sheep breeding was a valued industry and a revered culture of magic and medicine. The villagers trusted in the shepherd's ability to tend to the sheep, so that their bounty would sustain them through the long, cold winter.

The main character in herding sheep and farming was Ватаг, the elder shepherd. Ватаг oversaw the summer grazing of not only sheep, but all the livestock that needed to feed in the meadows. First of all, it had to be a senior shepherd who was well versed in folk rites, customs, rituals, and veterinary medicine. This experienced leader had earned great respect among the peasants, since he could protect livestock from the elements, accidents, and other animals. Ватаг selected shepherds at his own discretion and gave responsibilities to them. Some believed that Ватаг is both a sorcerer and a soother, for he knew how to survive long, hot days and withstand rainy nights, keeping both himself and the flock alive.

The shepherd reminds us that we must accept the changing path of our lives. While we may take part in habitual patterns, he is flexible when his direction suddenly shifts. He has patience and trusts that his work will create opportunities that will result in abundance for all.

6 OF AIR

Feeling: No compromise reached, transition in process, regrouping after a chaotic shake-up, making a choice.

Ask yourself: How can I look at difficult challenges in life with neutrality and without personal attachment?

Action: Reassess, regroup, and make a choice. Leave the storm and move to calmer waters.

Essence: When we remain true to our core values, then the choices we make in life are based on principles without compromise.

NOTES

Slender and beautiful from early life into maturity, the poplar represents both maiden beauty and sadness. She emanates modest feminine charm, but at the same time considerable resilience in her ability to bend but not break. She has a very delicate nature that is sensitive to the influence of age and its surrounding environment. It is also known that the poplar is able to free us from negative energy and, at the same time, clean the air of all evil, harmful, and wicked spirits.

Since the poplar has more-withered branches as it ages, she reminds us of how we age and take on increasingly more painful sorrows and burdens over time. That is why we often see the lonely poplar gathered among other trees of her kind for the companionship to withstand hardships that life may bring. The poplar does not like to grow alone and reminds us of how we need to be surrounded in community through the support and presence of family and friends.

It was under the poplar that the Evil One cradled the baby Judah, the future betrayer of Christ, on his lap. According to Ukrainian legend, the leaves of the tree trembled in agitation and apprehension over the presence of an unclean and uninvited guest in its shadow. The poplar's shivering branches stretched up from this place of discomfort toward the bright sky, fleeing from the disharmony of the "devil's lullaby."

The poplar is a mythical totem image of ancient Ukrainians. Held in late spring, the Poplar Festival is where the slimmest girl is chosen, with her hands gently bound above her head to symbolize the sacred tree. Ribbons, scarves, necklaces, and other adornments were hung on the raised hands as she was led through the village, field, and meadow as villagers sang, "Be flexible and strong; do not give in to the strong wind."

Legend says that if a girl could not be with the one who was meant for her, she would willingly choose to become the poplar, spending the rest of her life alone rather than unhappily with anyone else. The poplar trusts in her own resilience and flexibility to weather life's storms and challenges without compromise.

7 OF AIR

Feeling: Not knowing, seeking the truth, purity, going behind the veil to see the future, inquiring, guessing.

Ask yourself: Can I trust that life is unfolding in the way it is written in the stars?

Action: Shift the energy of "I need to know this now" to "Spirit, please show me the way and guide me to the next step."

Essence: When we force what is not ours, the most likely outcome is annoyance. The outcome will not be favorable.

NOTES

Magic floats up and around the fortune-teller, as she stands, dressed only in her night shift, illuminated only by a single candle. This gentle young woman knows nothing of her future, until she asks Andrew the First-Called to offer predictions and bring her good fortune. The candle glows and the mirror adds to the power of intuition, when maidens become fortune-tellers, with the help of the apostle Andrew.

The memorial day of Andrew the First-Called is one of the first holidays of the winter cycle. Ukrainian ancestors believed that real winter begins "on Andrew," and many traditions are associated with this Christian holiday, including those that the church has disavowed. Divination by Andrew has been condemned by the church since ancient times. Even today, priests ask parishioners not to try fortune-telling, but folk traditions are stronger than church prohibitions. For centuries, on the night of December 12 to 13, girls and women have been looking into the future. People believe that the night of Andrew the First-Called is full of magic.

Only on the night of December 13 do girls or women take part in fortune-telling. Before that, they must observe a fast, eating only bread and water and keeping strict silence until the morning after. The light goes out and the oldest girl is the first to tell fortunes. She adjusts to divination and mentally says, "Andrew, Andrew, show me my future destiny. Who shall I choose and what awaits me?"

Another rite is to stand naked in front of a mirror after six o'clock in the evening by the light of a candle. The young woman will turn around in front of the mirror and say, "I'm beautiful; I'm happy; I'll have my wish." On any days other than on Andrew's night, the magic of the mirror will take away both health and luck.

Fortune-telling is a sacred practice of the divine feminine. The fortune-teller brings a message of intuition and trust, as well as strong faith. It tells us that we have a connection to spirit and that knowledge that is ours will come naturally. What is not for us must be left unknown.

8 OF AIR

Feeling: Bad news, crisis, conflict, a feeling of being not in control, a feeling of being trapped.

Ask yourself: How can I relieve the pressure I feel in needing to achieve my desires?

Action: Be willing to look at difficult situations with a new lens that might be unfamiliar to me or uncomfortable.

Essence: When we are able to find moments to pause and find stillness, the path forward will present itself with absolute clarity.

NOTES

Traveling through the world of living and dead, the cat is both a guardian spirit and a harbinger of good. On the contrary, the cat is also a little demon, bringing harmful mischief and messages from the dark forces.

The cat can appear in colors of black or white. Witches or demons would often change form into a black cat to spy upon others. When the cat appears donning the color of the dark night on the road before any traveler, it is believed that misfortune would soon follow. Shamans say that to avert certain disaster, one was to throw a stick across the cat's trail so that the cat would follow in pursuit, diverted from the intended route of the traveler. In Ukraine, when there is a quarrel between two people, it is often said that a black cat has run between them.

The cat is very connected to the spiritual world, since he feels subtle shifts and changes in the mood of people and any fluctuations in the disposition of nature. Many believe that the cat can even see worlds invisible to the human eye. They see spirits and ghosts, as well as the past and the future, even into the afterlife. As such, the cat often accompanies those that live a life of magic as a companion and an indispensable partner in magical rites and mysteries. Cats were once recognized as such a loyal accomplice to witches that they were also burned together with their enchantress.

Traversing the fine line between good and evil, the cat has, over time, become known as a reliable protector and patron. At the same time, he also represents the darker servant of the devil.

The cat is a contradictory symbol, bringing both peace and quarrels to the house and continues to be a cross-border symbol that lives between the parallel realms of day and night.

9 OF AIR

Feeling: A call to faith, deep honoring of your roots, festivities, speaking out spells, calling in what you want for yourself and your community.

Ask yourself: How can I shift from loneliness to togetherness?

Action: Honor who you are and your ancestors. Authenticity is the power you carry from the earth, the land, the mother's womb.

Essence: When we deeply respect and cherish our ancestors' rites and customs, we pass on their wisdom through us to our lineage.

NOTES

The Star of Christmas, or Alatyr, shines with radiant color. This eight-pointed star boasts festive colors, gems, and ribbons as it decorates homes during the Christmas season. This traditional star is not only colorful, but beautiful in its symmetry, with each point reflected with one directly opposite. Bright and cheery, the Star of Christmas is the image of balance and harmony.

The Christmas Star, also called the Cross of Svarog, is a universal talisman that conveys the power and knowledge of ancestors. It symbolizes the harmonious relationship between the spiritual and the physical, the cosmic balance between creation and eternity, the harmony between heart and mind. If you put all the interpretations together, you can single out one common feature—a representation of the birth of life. In many cultures of the world, this symbol means God, the sun; in Ukrainian culture it is called the Star of Christmas.

Since the eight-pointed star is formed by superimposing a straight cross (feminine principle, the sun) and an oblique cross (masculine principle, the moon), the eight-pointed star symbolizes the beginning of all life on Earth and nature itself. The shape of the Alatyr is an octagram, which is ideologically a symbol of God, and a sign of order in the universe. It connects all sides of the world and denotes absolute balance.

Alatyr, in Slavic mythology, is a harbinger of God's goodness, the eye of creation. That is why the groups of carolers used the octagonal star as their main amulet and attribute of Christmas, dressing up in festive masks and skins of totem animals, glorifying the newborn sun.

The Alatyr is a symbol of balance, harmony, and faith. The Christmas Star honors traditions and roots of one's culture and community and asks that you honor your own authentic self.

10 OF AIR

Feeling: Abundance of Life—the connections, togetherness, celebration, deep reverence between human and God.

Ask yourself: How do I create closeness through the lens of true authenticity?

Action: Celebrate and express gratitude. You are worthy, and it is time to give yourself permission to enjoy the result of your creation.

Essence: When we adhere to our deepest sacred practices, we manifest the new beginnings with ease and grace.

NOTES

Under the pale winter sun, carolers share the joy of the Christmas season with friends and neighbors. Dressed in fine attire and cloaked in animal skins, the festive celebrants raise their voices in jubilant song in the crisp and sparkling winter night. One notable exception is the caroler dressed as a plain gray goat, like Kolyada's[1] clever camouflage that saved her from Marena.[2] Carrying their colorful token, the Star of Christmas,[3] this merry group leaves the warmth of the hearth and the nourishment of their feast, to sing traditional Christmas songs for all to hear.

The main Ukrainian celebrations of New Year's and Christmas begin when the winter sun turns to summer sun, after the winter solstice on the twenty-first of December.

Before the holiday, Ukrainians sew new embroidered shirts for each member of the family to bring good fortune for the next year. A fire is lit as a symbol of the birth of a new sun. Ukrainians will sprinkle each other and their houses with grain, to bring a good harvest. They burn a log that symbolizes the evil Marena, and they all eat Kutia, a traditional Christmas dish. After the Holy Supper, they sing carols, dressed in ceremonial costumes. Christmas carols are majestic ritual songs of the winter holiday, originating from ancient times. These traditional songs proclaim and spread blessings of the Christmas holiday among people, complete with its mysticism and its religious content. The basis of this reverence is to celebrate the creation of the world. It marks a new beginning for all people, blessed by loved ones and community.

Carols used to be pagan songs, against which the Orthodox Church initially waged an unsuccessful struggle to ban them. However, Kolyada rites proved to be very stable in Ukraine, marked in many ways by the features of pagan beliefs, reminiscent of honoring both the newborn sun and the traditions of ancestors.

The tradition of Christmas caroling is one that connects us with others, with joy and celebration. This is the season of new beginnings. This tradition reminds us to express gratitude and celebration for our gifts. With faith and purity of thought, we may manifest new beginnings with ease and grace.

---

1. Kolyada—Ace of Air
2. Marena—Major Arcana #13
3. Star of Christmas—9 of Air

Minor Arcana
Water

Ace of Water

Feeling: Pure joy, satisfaction on an emotional level, nourishment, true heart, fertility, felicity.

Ask yourself: How do I nourish myself and expand my capacity to become a conduit for abundance?

Action: Pour from your heart all the love you have; do not hold anything back.

Essence: When we give from an open and expansive heart, the energy of abundance flows through us and to us.

Notes

Draped in velvet and satin, Yarylo (Ярило) smiles with warmth and joy. The sun god's face is radiant as he toys with the magic of the great golden sphere. Yarylo's perfection may be glimpsed in his entire being, proving that he is proud to bring his magnitude of light.

The glorious Yarylo is the god of abundance and light, and he came into the world to give people a bright day, to share with them their happiness, fate, kindness, and love. As the son of the great Svarog,[1] he is the giver of all good, the guardian of human destiny and wealth. Yarylo also stands vigilantly guarding the laws of ancestors. He has been called the Grandfather Who Knows Everything because he sees everything and knows everything.

As legend goes, Yarylo the Sun was born from Kolyada,[2] the goddess of light, through her golden egg. From those ancient times, he has been said to create life with a particle of red blood in every egg. That is why, since early times, Easter eggs[3] have been painted in red and written on in front of a living fire. This practice was considered the highest charm against evil spirits. Once the eggs were consumed, the shells were highly regarded as prayers and were given back to Mother Earth in honor of this ritual of bounty and protection.

When Yarylo arrives during the spring equinox, the bread makers[4] turn to the god of abundance and light, asking for prosperity and earthly fruits. The highest prayer was asking for a rich bounty during the harvest.

Like the sun in the sky, Yarylo brings warmth and joy to those who behold him. Since he shares his bountiful gifts indiscriminately, we feel that we are all worthy of God's given blessings. From here, we create and share more abundance and love.

---

1. Svarog—Major Arcana #4
2. Kolyada—Ace of Air
3. Easter egg—9 of Water
4. Bread maker—5 of Earth

Page of Water

Feeling: Tender and delicate spiritual beauty, righteousness and holiness, purity of soul, elegance, modesty, and kindness. A humble reminder of nature's beauty.

Ask yourself: How can I add playfulness and childlike wonder to my life? What would be the first step toward finding the love and intimacy that my heart is longing for?

Action: Open your heart fully. Accept the beginning of intimacy and allow new relationships to bloom!

Essence: Surrender and trust that your soulmate is on their way.

Notes

Gathered with its brothers and sisters, the tender cornflower reflects the blue sky above. The cornflower is simple, elegant, and inviting to the eye and the heart. She emanates the innocence of love through nature's simplicity.

The cornflower is one of the twelve flowers of the Ukrainian wreath, and a symbol of the spiritual beauty of our people. As a symbol of the promise of newfound love, cornflowers portray the contrast of boyish beauty and kindness, and girlish modesty and tenderness. A cornflower infusion is magical and is sprinkled on lawns, where boys and girls walk together to enhance the essence of romance in the air.

On the outskirts of the Ukraine, legend tells of a mermaid that seduced a beautiful blue-eyed young man named Vasylko. She entranced him with her captivating beauty and led him out to a field of rye. He followed her for an entire week, enchanted by her charms, and longed to experience a happy moment of love with her.

But the mermaid did not let Vasylko approach her, for fear he would discover who she was. When he realized the futility of the pursuit, Vasylko attempted to turn back. She caught him at the edge of the field and, afraid of losing him forever, cast a spell, turning him into a beautiful flower that matched the shade of his blue eyes.

The cornflower is now a sacred flower of the mermaid. It is said that mermaids jealously watch over the cornflowers until they lose all color and turn gray.

The cornflower is a symbol of life, youth, beauty, modesty, and simplicity. This flower reminds us of childlike wonder, the virtue of new love. The cornflower invites us to trust that our soulmate is on their way and that love is ready to bloom.

Messenger of Water

Feeling: The arrival of love, romantic attraction, admiration, sweetness of freedom and pleasure coming to your life.

Ask yourself: How would my life change if I choose to connect on a deeper emotional level?

Action: Open yourself with vulnerability to the world you live in, approaching everything and everyone with love as your first intention.

Essence: Living a sincere life connected to the universe with an open heart allows us to receive the abundance of its love in return.

Notes

The nightingale is a songstress, full of beauty and innocence. Her shining feathers and dainty song enhance the power of her allure. She is considered the messenger of romantic attraction, and a symbol of freedom and renewal.

The nightingale is often mentioned in Ukrainian love songs and has become known as a bird of lovers, revered by Slavic peoples. The universe encouraged the courtship of young people by sending the nightingale to trill her happy song as a sign, enveloping young lovers as they weave the soul's tapestry of their newfound attraction. The absence of a nightingale's song indicates a premonition of trouble and a suggestion for them to continue their search for the perfect soulmate.

Nightingales did not live on our lands, since they nested in distant countries unaware of Ukraine. The tiny birds would swiftly fly across all nations, gathering songs from around the world, bringing them back to Lada's[1] garden. On one such trip, a nightingale came to rest in a small Ukrainian village. While the nightingale paused, she heard the magical songs of Ukraine's people and was awestruck. In all her journeys, she had never heard such moving lyrical songs that spoke of the people's love of Mother Earth, the courage and bravery of the Ukrainian spirit, and the wisdom of Ukraine's ancestors.

The nightingale learned the songs of Ukraine and brought them back to Lada. The goddess was so enamored with the beautiful melodies that she asked the nightingale to continue singing the songs, day and night. From that day forward, nightingales have flown to Ukraine each spring to hear the songs, translate them into their own sweet melody, and sing them anew for Lada.

The nightingale sings of love and harmony and is a timeless testament to the blissful union of two consummate souls. She knows that love shared freely with the purest of intentions will always be multiplied and returned manyfold. She generously shares her gift of song and encourages us to give ours from the heart and be open to its beautiful requite.

---

1. Lada—Major Arcana #3

Queen of Water

Feeling: Compassionate, calm, intuitive, and devoted. The one who offers service, takes care of others, and has natural healing abilities.

Ask yourself: How do I find balance between caring for myself and giving to others?

Action: Find love and compassion for yourself as you would for others.

Essence: When we practice abundant love for ourselves, we become fully capable to love and serve others.

Notes

Eupraksia Mstislavivna was an ancient Ukrainian княгиня,[1] the first female doctor, pharmacist, and scientist in the history of Kyivan Rus. She became the empress of Byzantium and the first woman to have published a medical text.

Since childhood, Eupraksia was interested in the secrets of folk medicine and studied the properties of healing plants and ointments. As an adult, she chose to offer treatment to those who were less fortunate. Because of her philanthropy and love of people, Eupraksia was called Добродія, which translates as "She Who Does Good Deeds."

Historically, women who practiced folk medicine were suspected of sorcery and witchcraft. Due to Eupraksia's generous and compassionate heart, she never had to deal with such judgment.

In the Byzantine Empire, medical science was quite developed, with numerous medical texts already written and the first hospitals having been established at monasteries. By marrying the Byzantine king, Oleksiy Komnenos, the union offered her the opportunity to further her medical education.

On the basis of her own experience and analysis of modern research, Eupraksia wrote a Greek paper called "Ointment," which was highly regarded in the medical community. Despite its modest name, this study became an encyclopedia of medical knowledge, combining modern and historical medical literature with personal experience and deep critical analysis. The study was celebrated for its clarity and simplicity and remains relevant even to this day.

Not only was Eupraksia a groundbreaking medical scientist, but she will also always be remembered for her kind heart and willingness to help those who were unable to afford medical services. She also left a legacy of female leadership in the field of medicine.

---

1. Княгиня is a historical Slavic title, used both as a royal and noble title, and is usually translated into English as princess or duchess.

King of Water

Feeling: Diplomatic, fair, mediator, peacemaker, emotionally balanced.

Ask yourself: How do I stay calm and stop my emotions from overtaking my decision-making?

Action: Observe your feelings objectively and accept them without allowing them to control you. This will allow you to choose emotionally balanced responses with diplomacy.

Essence: When we draw upon our emotional maturity and stability, we have a higher capacity to navigate life's challenges.

Notes

Великий князь[1] Danylo Halytskyi was one of the brightest historical figures of the Middle Ages. He was a powerful ruler, a shrewd politician and diplomat, and a brave warrior and commander. Danylo Halytskyi was the last Великий князь of Ukraine and the first and only king on our lands. He was considered to be an outstanding commander and public figure, as demonstrated by how the Galicia-Volhynia state was at the peak of its economic, cultural, and diplomatic development during his reign.

Великий князь lived in a stormy, brutal era of civil strife and Mongol-Tatar raids. He was a brave, fearless fighter blessed with great skills of mediation and negotiation. Danylo was recognized for successfully bringing an end to the dependence on the Mongol-Tatar conquerors. The successful struggle of Danylo Halytskyi against the Mongol-Tatars created a precedent of victories over the previously invincible troops of the Golden Horde.

Danylo Halytskyi also played a significant role in the history of a particularly memorable siege upon the Polish city of Kalisz. He personally breached the city walls, disguised as a common citizen, covering his face with a dull helmet. After hearing the townspeople debate the merits of whether to surrender to the invading army, Великий князь Danylo went to the center of the gathering and announced himself. He then offered that the city surrender to him personally. The Poles, impressed by such courage and nobility, agreed and bargained a peace treaty with the brave warrior.

Великий князь Danylo Halytskyi was fifty-two years old at the time of coronation, and his state was one of the largest in Europe at the time. This event led to the integration of the Volyn land, as part of the Galicia-Volhynia state, into the European community. Danylo Halytskyi became the only Ukrainian ruler who received the title of king and became a full-fledged European monarch.

---

1. Великий князь is the ruler of a great state or an autonomous great principality. Usually translates as grand duke to distinguish him from the other dukes.

2 OF WATER

Feeling: Trust and infinite love, soul connection, harmony in relationships, full satisfaction of desires, purity.

Ask yourself: How can I enhance heart-to-heart connection in all relationships?

Action: Start creating interdependent relationships, since this will lead to long-lasting and mutually satisfying connections.

Essence: When we recognize that God is at the heart of all relationships, it is our duty to tend to them with love, tenderness, and reverence.

NOTES

Dressed in the finery of the Ukrainian tradition, the groom embraces the hand of his bride. Soulmates are joined in matrimony, their fingers entwined, a symbol of the bond of love for all to see.

The Ukrainian folk wedding is one of the most ancient and complex ceremonies in the system of family rituals. It holds a spiritual component of our culture and carries tremendous history into the present day. In the custom of our ancestors, the great traditional Ukrainian wedding is divided into separate ceremonies, each with its own ritual songs, traditional foods, and ritual breads. Thousand-year-old prayers, melodies, majestic hymns, and spiritually deep rituals are interwoven into the creation of this new family.

The purpose of the wedding ceremony is to create a stronger family; since the ancestral circles of the young man and young woman are bound through this marriage, the two families become one.

The bride and groom are regarded as soulmates, a divine couple. Strong and capable, they are endowed with the sacred gift of continuing the lineage and must bring into the coming ages numerous offspring. During the wedding, these young people give special gifts to one another. According to tradition, the bride presents the young man with an embroidered shirt, which carries the spiritual wealth, high wisdom, and traditional connection of many generations. This gift is said to influence and invoke health, beauty, prosperity, and family fidelity. It has long been believed that the embroidered shirt offers protection from evil spirits.

The young man graciously presents the bride with soft boots as a promise that she will never walk barefoot. The boots represent a commitment to protect his wife and to always provide for her.

The Ukrainian wedding ceremony is a symbol of unity and love. It reminds us that all good things come from interdependence on this earth. Trust, connection, and relationships all are vital for our greatest desires to come to fruition.

3 OF WATER

Feeling: Joy, togetherness, good times, happiness, cheerfulness, contentment.

Ask yourself: How do I express my gratitude for the richness of the life I live?

Action: Open your heart to a joyful celebration of each moment of life. Do not wait; each moment is precious.

Essence: When we realize that we are a part of something bigger, we act in unity and create more coherence in the universe. Together, we raise the vibration of joy and gratitude.

NOTES

With his mallets balanced gently in his fingers, the musician strikes the strings of the tsymbaly, sending rich and cheerful notes into the world. Although he is deeply engaged in the creation of music, the player of the tsymbaly shares the joy of the melody as it drifts off the beautiful gold strings.

The tsymbaly is a stringed musical instrument consisting of a wooden body and strings stretched over it. Usually, the upper part of the instrument is made of spruce, and the lower part is made of sycamore. As music is produced by striking the strings with a stick or mallet, the spirit of the trees is carried through the air, inspiring joyful dancing.

The tsymbaly is considered to be the oldest of musical instruments and represents joy for life and celebration of community and friendship. For a long period of time, the tsymbaly was one of the main instruments of what is known as "Triple Musicians"—an early Ukrainian ensemble that provided musical accompaniment at weddings, baptisms, holidays, and other folk festivities.

The ensembles performed mainly dance and song melodies. That is probably why the tsymbaly is usually mentioned in a common context with the history of Ukrainian choreography, since they always inspire our Ukrainian souls to a cheerful dance!

The tsymbaly is a unique instrument with rich musical imagery. The instrument's bright and clear yet gentle and long-lasting bell-like sound is extremely pleasant to the ear.

Such a happy song emanates from the tsymbaly, reminding us that now is the time for gratitude and celebration. Open your heart to joy, since each moment is precious. Do not wait for a special occasion; the time for celebration is now.

4 OF WATER

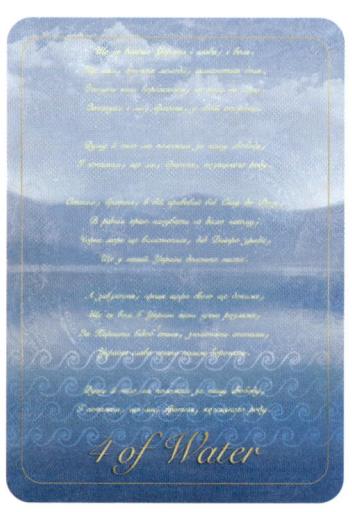

Feeling: Abounding in song, melodious flow, arising from the heart.

Ask yourself: How can I stop allowing my negative thoughts to influence decisions I make in my life?

Action: Feel the feelings as they come, and do not deny them even if they are not immediately serving you.

Essence: When we embody what is without any judgment and justification, we allow the flow of life to move through us and for us.

NOTES

The anthem of Ukraine is one of our most paramount symbols, emboldening its people. More than just words or music, it reveals the strength, essence, and meaning of the state and its aspirations. Eliciting emotions of an awakened and vibrant spirit, the anthem summates the ideology and goals of a nation: Be free and cause no harm to others, since we are a peaceful and cheerful nation.

The anthem encourages respect for individual rights and basic freedom. It speaks to the core principles of the constitution that Ukraine is a peaceful state that does not wish anyone harm, and it is a nation of courage and freedom whose power and resolve shall not be deterred.

> Ukraine's freedom has not perished
> nor has her glory gone.
> Once again, all Ukraine's
> fate will smile upon.
> Enemies will perish
> like dew in the sun.
> We shall possess, all my people,
> a free land of our own.
> We will lay down soul and body
> and show that we are one.
> We will stand together for our freedom;
> none shall rule our home.
> Ukraine's freedom has not perished
> nor has her glory gone.
> We will stand together for our freedom;
> none shall rule our home.[1]

The anthem reminds us of the merit in observing neutrality in all events. Being able to withhold judgment gives us the freedom and power to allow the flow of the human spirit to carry us beyond any challenge or fear that should stand in our way.

---

1. Patti Smith, translation from Ukraine into English, 2022.

5 OF WATER

Feeling: Freedom, expression, innovation, releasing, surrendering, forgiveness.

Ask yourself: How do I allow my true self to express itself without reservation?

Action: Surrender to what is, and express your sincere emotions as they arise.

Essence: When we freely allow our spirit to express itself, we become a part of the current of life.

NOTES

The amazing ornamental painting of the people of Petrykivka[1] is one of the vivid manifestations of Ukrainian art. Petrykivka dances in the hearts and minds of the people of Ukraine, its vibrant colors as diverse as its creators.

The Petrykivka is often based on elements of nature, such as lush viburnum berries, songbirds, flowers, and foliage. The process of painting these works becomes a spiritual exercise. As the Petrykivka starts to unfold, the hand of the artist begins to take on a life of its own, and its spirit becomes the painter expressing directly from the heart.

Petrykivka is a village of artists—everyone paints and produces stunning pieces of art. They draw on wood or paint walls, stoves, furniture, dishes, or any other object as a canvas. Fairy-tale firebirds fly from lacquered plates and vases, red viburnum reach for the skies, and lush ferns bloom with Kupala[2] flowers.

Many researchers have tied the mystery of the Petrykivka painting to ancient things that once belonged to Zaporozhian Cossacks.[3] There was never serfdom in the village of Petrykivka, since it was a place of Cossack's winter quarters. The town's inhabitants felt secure and safe in this place, protected by the people's army. Therefore, people were free in their thoughts and creativity, so artisans spent time and energy in flow, creating, innovating, and expressing their innermost emotions through art.

Petrykivka is more than a traditional art form. It is an invitation to release burdens and surrender to trust and forgiveness. Creativity blossoms when there is a free-flowing current of guidance, rooted in truth. The Petrykivka is an everlasting symbol embodying how to let your creative emotions take flight in all of your endeavors.

---

1. Petrykivka painting or simply "Petrykivka"—a traditional Ukrainian decorative painting style, originating from the village of Petrykivka, Ukraine. It is a part of the intangible cultural heritage and is included in the UNESCO Representative List of the Intangible Cultural Heritage of Humanity.
2. Night of Ivana Kupala—10 of Fire
3. Cossack—Major Arcana #8

6 OF WATER

Feeling: Resilience, flexibility, hope, a sense of belonging, and safety. Nostalgia about past happiness, reflection on childhood.

Ask yourself: Am I stuck moving forward because I am absorbed with regrets of the past?

Action: Be here now. Let go of emotional connections to the past that are holding you back from living fully in the present.

Essence: When we live intentionally in the present moment, it gives us the power to look upon the past with graciousness.

NOTES

The willow's delicate leaves cascade toward the crystalline pond, drinking in her reflection along with the nourishing water. Behind the lush green curtain of her tender branches stands a trunk strong enough to bear weight, but supple enough to sway in the strongest wind. She is an alluring contrast both of resilient durability and graceful suppleness.

She is a strong and flexible mother, full of practicality and mystery. The tree is endowed with a sense of nostalgia for the past, with strong memories of childhood. The willow is a symbol of belonging and protection.

The willow is the sacred tree of the Slavs, not only as a symbol of Ukraine but also as a ritual and medicinal plant. People say that willow can relieve headaches, treat infertility, heal wounds, and take away negative energy. The sacred willow was also widely used in various magical rites and everyday life. With the willow branch, storm clouds were dispersed, cattle were driven out to pasture, fires were extinguished, and water was sought for a newfound well.

The willow branches are also kept in homes as a reminder of God's presence. The Gospel story says that when Jesus Christ raised Lazarus from the dead, people believed that he was truly the Son of God. Many met Jesus to honor him at the entrance to Jerusalem and paved the way for him with palm branches. At this time in Ukraine, only the sacred willow blooms so she was chosen for consecration. After many hundreds of years, people still bring twigs of the willow to the church in memory of this event.

The willow is a softhearted sentimental tree of nostalgia and reminiscence. She allows for a moment of reflection but tenderly moves us away from living in the past so that we can move forward to living a purposeful life in the present.

7 OF WATER

Feeling: New things are coming; possibilities and choices to be made; visioning; inspiration; planning.

Ask yourself: How can I become unstuck from having an infinite number of choices?

Action: Close your eyes and imagine the most positive of outcomes, then proceed with this vision as your purpose.

Essence: When we clearly see what our true desire is, the universe will respond to our heart's desire in reality.

NOTES

On a peaceful shore beside a still river, young maidens weave colorful floral wreaths. Romance and magic are in the air, enveloping the lush meadow where a host of hopeful girls are gathered. This sisterhood comes together to craft a perfect wreath of colorful blooms. Each garland represents and holds their personal dreams and wishes. As they gather near the water, a sense of tranquil, peaceful joy arises as the young maidens don their blossoming crowns of womanhood.

The custom of weaving wreaths is a spring tradition that has been with us since ancient times. The ceremony of weaving the flower crown usually would start on Green holidays, which lasted a whole week, marking the end of the spring and the beginning of summer. The flowered crown is our Holy Soul of Immortality and the secret of procreation, prosperity, and wealth. Fresh flowers, most suited to a young girl's face, were cornflowers, periwinkle, saffron, lovage, and motherwort, woven together into potent rings of love awash in nature's vibrant colors.

"To wear a wreath is to love life" are words that came to us from the ancestral Ukrainians. In those days, a crown made of flowers, ears of corn, and berries not only was a symbol of female passion but was also an honorary tribute to the goddess Mokosha,[1] Mother Earth. At a time of transition from a girl's family to her mate, this woven circle of fragrant blooms marks a significant time for girls reclaiming their soul and their full potential.

The flower crown is a physical manifestation of youthful hopes and dreams, as well as their fulfillment. The flower crown reminds us to imagine the most resplendent tomorrow and to weave these aspirations into reality. Believe in the magic of your vision to create an inspired reality in your future.

---

1. Mokosha—Ace of Earth

8 OF WATER

Feeling: Rooting down in wisdom, trusting creation, honoring prophecies that you cannot escape.

Ask yourself: How can I let go of attachments to outcomes that limit the unfolding?

Action: Find courage to walk away from situations that don't serve you.

Essence: When we trust that we are where we are meant to be, we allow life to flow with ease and confidence.

NOTES

The snake moves in the Tree of Life[1] in a continual state of transformation. The tree, with its crown (the heavenly sphere), trunk (the earthly world), and roots (underground depths), magically cocreates with the snake. The snake is considered an untouchable sacred being that is blessed with magical properties.

Snakes are typically found nestling under the roots of the wise oaks,[2] since they are comfortable in the shade of the underworld, embodying evil power.

In Ukrainian folklore, there is a beautiful tale that speaks to how releasing someone or something important to you will not alter your destiny.

Shamans prophesied to Oleg[3] that he would die from his beloved horse.[4] Oleg ordered the horse to be freed to avoid the fulfillment of the prophecy. Years later, Oleg was told that his trusty steed had passed. At first, he laughed at the wise man's prophecy, for here he was, still alive and well. However, he grew sentimental and elected to visit the horse's grave. There, he discovered that there were only bones remaining of his once-beloved companion. However, his conceit overtook him as he put his foot on the skull and cried out, "Should I be afraid of him?" At that very moment, the snake living in the skull of the horse sprang and sunk his poisonous fangs into Oleg, thereby proving the prophecy to be true and also taking his life.

Both a revered and sometimes feared creature, the snake is a vibrant spirit, as well as a protector. As the lord of the waters and underground fire, the snake continues to play a major role in the creation of the world and personification of its elements. The snake teaches us the power of surrender and that life unfolds with greater ease when we lose our desire to control it.

---

1. Tree of Life—Major Arcana #21
2. Oak—6 of Earth
3. князь Oleg Vischchy was the first to begin the unification of East Slavic tribes into a single state, Kyivan Rus, and made Kyiv the "mother of Kyivan Rus cities" in 912. His death is described in the Tale of Bygone Years.
4. Horse—8 of Fire

9 OF WATER

Feeling: Contentment, enjoying the holy magical process of creating, communicating feelings and frequencies through the magic.

Ask yourself: Have I been paying attention to how I express my emotions and thoughts?

Action: Make a conscious effort when communicating, since words are spells that carry frequencies, encoding your fate.

Essence: When the seed of intention is planted from a pure heart, we experience not only emotional satisfaction but also our wish comes true, since it is aligned with a higher purpose.

NOTES

The decorative Easter egg (Pysanka) is written and colored with sacred symbols and designs. Its beautiful shell shines with a smooth luster over its painted surface. The delicately inscribed lines and shapes of the Pysanka weave a magic spell during the holiest of days, blending artwork, tradition, and magic into this timeless gem.

Pysanka is the main attribute of Великдень.[1] With great solemnity and prayers, women began this sacred ceremony of writing on eggs with ancient coded magical symbols. They are mainly geometric: triangles, spirals, circles, clovers, and branches. All these are signs of various rituals or sacred numbers.

Our ancestors identified Pysanka as the universe, from which the sky and the earth originate. In the middle, where the yolk sits, the sun symbolically arises. The ornament of the Easter egg carries secret knowledge and messages from the past, through the unique drawings and signs encoded onto their surface. The symbols on Pysanka are messages from the past, instructions, and bequests to posterity and harmony of the universe.

Many magical actions were performed with Easter eggs. To ensure a bountiful harvest, the eggs were rolled over green wheat and buried in the ground. On Easter morning, young people washed themselves with water, in which they had previously put eggs and silver coins, believing that this would bring them strength and beauty. Sacred Easter eggs protected the home from thunder and fire, or from people, animals, and the "evil eye."

The Ukrainian Pysanka is not only a means of communication with people, but also a means of communication with God, through prayer.

The writing and painting of Pysanka have long been purposeful and sacred actions, meant to communicate with our loved ones and with God. The Pysanka reminds us that all actions bring magic, with presence, purpose, and love. Everything we experience is happening for us and through us. Be present and grateful for the opportunity to express through blessed and purposeful communication.

---

1. Великдень—10 of Water

10 OF WATER

Feeling: Family and community connections, abundance, celebration, joy.

Ask yourself: How do I keep my mind, body, and spirit open for heartfelt connections and experiences?

Action: Mindfulness and rituals of purification invite more space for what I want to attract in my life.

Essence: When we honor and adhere to generational wisdom and traditions, we become conduits for abundance to flow.

NOTES

The spring sun peeks through the buds of the cherry tree, warming the air and the earth while joyful celebration commences. The Easter holiday is bright and cheery, filled with singing, dancing, and bonding among community. The smiles on the faces of young and old reflect the joy of spring and the hope for the future.

Ukrainians refer to the Easter holiday as Velykden (Великдень), which translates to "Big Sunny Day." Velykden sits on the east of the Ukrainian shamanic wheel in the spring of the year and represents the sunrise, fire, and the action. This is a day when the magic of fertility prevails, as Yarylo,[1] god of abundance, goodness, light, and vitality, warms the earth and watches over it.

The essence of this traditional holiday was marked by unique and rich rituals including the celebration of willow,[2] painting Easter eggs, and baking Easter bread. It is a celebration of the spring sun and the rebirth of nature. This holiday embraces the victory of light over darkness and day over night.

Velykden captures the magic of bonding together, as family, as community, and as spiritual beings. This celebration begins on Pure Thursday, when everything in the household is cleaned, polished, and purified, including members of the family. On Good Friday, Easter bread is baked for good health and igniting the heart. Christians eventually dedicated this day to the suffering of the physical body of Christ through fasting. Saturday is a day of silence and introspection, while women complete preparations for the Velykden celebrations, including the writing of Pysanka, the Easter egg. Finally, on Easter Sunday, shutters are thrown wide open, welcoming the sun, with all its abundance and happiness. This is the celebration of hope, reminiscent of the Christian celebration of Jesus rising from the dead. Family and friends gather for huge morning feasts to express love and gratitude for the past year and to make wishes for abundance and joy until the next Velykden.

Великдень celebrates traditions and rituals of gratitude and joy. It is a reminder that darkness cannot last, just as the sun brings an end to the night. Good things are always available, with mindful practices, pure actions, and strong faith.

---

1. Yarylo—Ace of Fire
2. Willow tree—6 of Water

MINOR ARCANA
FIRE

ACE OF FIRE

Feeling: Celebration, spirit-powered action, new opportunities, original source of action. Money, fortune, inheritance, creation, invention, enterprise, family.

Ask yourself: How can I infuse my life with joy and cheerfulness so I can inspire myself and others to follow their dreams?

Action: Be bold, take risks, go on an adventure, and believe in yourself.

Essence: When we ignite the fire within, this potent and powerful energy will illuminate the path.

NOTES

Kupala rests in the mossy forest, embracing the beautiful Flower of the Magic Fern. His handsome face beams with joy and celebration, while he takes in the enchanted bloom. Charming and cheerful, this god of the rising sun requires no finery in order to shine.

Kupala—god of the highest rising sun—represents the summer solstice, the summit, and the uniter of opposites. He is the highest manifestation of love, a guardian and protector of married couples, and is associated with the elements of water and fire. Kupala is a connoisseur and a connector, whose strength lies in his mature frenzy and awareness of the unity of all living things.

It is Kupala that lights the Flower of the Magic Fern, the fiery flower of happiness and manifestation! Our ancestors were fascinated and sometimes possessed with the idea of finding this magical flower, believing that it could help them create everything that they desired. However, this blossom is shown only to those whose intentions are pure.

On the eve of Ivana Kupala,[1] the most-sacred rites and actions are held because Kupala's sun is at its zenith. At this time, the trees can walk and herbs can talk, since they are celebrating the beautiful time of creation and love! On Kupala, the gates of heaven are opened and all glorifications fly easily and freely to the gods.

Kupala tells us that anything is possible. Dreams and aspirations take flight, under this bright sun, so they have the courage to venture into the unknown. Believe in yourself; you will be blessed.

---

1. Night of Ivana Kupala—Ace of Fire

Page of Fire

Feeling: Power and strength, positive energy, warmth, happiness, joy, optimism, eternal gratitude.

Ask yourself: How can I infuse power into my new endeavors? What is stopping me from dreaming big and taking bold actions?

Action: Ignite your purposeful light by expressing gratitude for your life's blessings.

Essence: When we give reverence and gratitude to our life experiences, we bring forth our own light into the world.

Notes

The hearty marigold is both beautiful and strong, with warmth shining from its rippling petals. Marigolds are an infinite tender tie to Mother Earth and our own mothers. Its gold and orange hues remind us of a mother's love and bring forth a vision of her caring hands.

In Ukrainian culture the marigold is a national symbol of childhood, our native mother, father, and home. They are symbolic of the Ukrainian hostesses' love of planting flowers by intricately weaving the medicine of herbs and flowers as the mystical fairies of the land. The traditional summer fast, Spásivka,[1] features the marigold in the ritual bouquet that holds feminine energy of our lineage and helps bring blessings throughout the year.

Legend speaks of how the marigold came to be. A long time ago, Ukraine knew of no trouble. It was a time when singing people peacefully baked bread, welcoming everyone who came with good intentions. It was a fertile, luminous landscape with green meadows, rich forests, and blue rivers. Over time, foreigners arrived carrying heavy grief and tears with them. They came with intentions to capture the mothers' most precious young Ukrainian boys, who would grow up to become strong men and their obedient slaves.

When the invaders approached the settlement, the mothers sought help from an old grandmother of the village who was their healer.[2] It was said that she knew of magic to protect their beloved sons. "Stay near your mothers," said the old woman just as she spoke her spell, and all the boys turned into splendorous, bushy, black-bearded, and brown-eyed flowers wrapped around her feet.

To this day, the marigold blossoms until late fall, representing the lasting unity of house and mother. There is no Ukraine without a white house and marigolds. It is the bloom that caresses the mother's heart until autumn's first frost.

---

1. Spásivka—9 of Fire
2. Hierophant—Major Arcana #5

Messenger of Fire

Feeling: Eternal awakening, resurrection and rebirth, headstrong certitude, beginnings.

Ask yourself: Which areas of my life are calling for bravery and action to start anew? What is possible when I call upon my inner courage and determination?

Action: Rise and shine! It is time to act! Awaken with confidence and nobility. Move forward by taking initiative toward realizing your dreams.

Essence: I choose to be the one who takes the first steps, bringing light and possibility into each new day.

Notes

Handsome, bold, and confident, the rooster is a revered bird, watchman, and keeper of universal time. He sings in unison with nature and ushers in the bright light of a new dawn. Rooster sits in neutrality through the dark night, with a strong sense of knowing when the sun will rise again. As the first sunrays appear on the horizon, the rooster's crow lets the world know that darkness has passed and that it is time to bask in the healing warmth of the new day.

Grandfathers in Ukraine have long told the story of the rooster. The rooster was called Kochet, and one day he laid a magic egg. From this egg flowed seven rivers that filled the earth with lush and vibrant plants. The world became a paradise, and soon it was filled with carefree and joyful people. Kochet sat high in the sky, and every day he called out to the people to remind them of their daily tasks to keep them well and happy. As an ever-diligent watcher of time, the rooster would also remind them of when to undertake these tasks.

God's people soon grew tired of the repeated noise, and they asked him to free them of this annoying bird. "We are already aware of what to do and when to do it." The Creator listened and fulfilled the people's request. When the divine rooster disappeared from the sky, the natural order was soon fractured, and thereafter hunger and disease afflicted the world. At Easter, people now write on eggs to call for the return of the heavenly rooster to be reborn and to restore order to the earth and its people.

The rooster wears a crown and bright plumage to remind us of our own power and nobility. His song awakens a courage within each of us to march out of the restful darkness into the light, where our passions and dreams exist to be recognized, acted upon, and fulfilled.

Queen of Fire

Feeling: Independent, fiery, courageous, lovely, humorous, enticing, and magnetic.

Ask yourself: How can I unbind my passions to daringly move forward without fear of failure?

Action: Be courageous to step into a more powerful version of yourself to engage and lead others.

Essence: When we allow our vibrant spirit to express itself fully, we inspire others and give them permission to do the same.

Notes

Over half a century ago, a young Ukrainian girl, Anastasia Lisovska, was kidnapped as a slave to the Ottoman Empire, where she would eventually become the great Roksolana. She is historically remembered as the brightest ruler of the Ottoman Empire, and the wife of the most recognized sultan, Suleiman the Magnificent.

Songs have been sung of the girl kidnapped into Suleiman's harem, where her beauty and charms slowly won him over. He became monogamous in his affections for her, and she became the only concubine ever to marry a sultan. Anastasia was appointed the new name of Roksolana (woman from Kyivan Rus) and the nickname Hurrem (laughing) Sultan.

Roksolana learned the ways of Persian culture, and her determination made her a worthy rival of Suleiman's trusted advisors. Her political savvy became evident since she was extremely intelligent and well educated. Roksolana participated in numerous matters of state and local affairs. Her legacy leaves behind numerous charities, schools, and religious buildings across the empire. So successful was she that many other leaders could attribute it only to being witchcraft at work.

When Roksolana passed, the sultan ordered a rosary to be planted around her, and a luxurious tomb was placed over her. So inconsolable was Suleiman the Magnificent that he composed this poem for his wife:

Throne of my lonely niche, my wealth, my love, my moonlight. My most sincere friend, my confidant, my very existence, my Sultan, my one and only love.

The most beautiful among the beautiful . . .

My springtime, my merry-faced love, my daytime, my sweetheart, laughing leaf . . . my plants, my sweet, my rose, the one only who does not distress me in this world . . .

My woman of the beautiful hair, my love of the slanted brow, my love of eyes full of mischief . . .

I, lover of the tormented heart, Muhibbi, of the eyes full of tears, I am happy.

Roksolana remains an eminent figure in history. She lived up to her life mission, ensuring that the Ottoman Empire would never strike against the people of Ukraine. She is a Ukrainian woman who will forever be recognized as a legendary pioneer of bravery, courage, and independence that changed the course of history.

King of Fire

Feeling: Passionate, noble, powerful, resilient, influencer, visionary mindful leader.

Ask yourself: How can I find inspiration from the beauty that exists in my life?

Action: Seek out and continue to foster creativity within.

Essence: When we honor the passion in our heart, we can persevere toward what is to come.

Notes

Гетьман[1] Ivan Mazepa was the most popular Ukrainian hetman in history for his passion for culture, coupled with his love of his people. He was a great patron of cultural initiatives and buildings in Ukraine. The development of fine arts, especially architecture, is most impressive during Mazepa's time. The city of Kyiv was reborn as the spiritual center of Ukraine through his influence.

The Mazepyn era was a time of flourishing cultural life of Ukrainian hetmanate. In music, the Ukrainian baroque attained its highest levels of affluence during Mazepa's time. Ivan Mazepa also generously financed the development of domestic science, education, art, and book printing.

Гетьман Mazepa was a statesman and politician of the highest regard. He was one of the most famous and skilled hetmans in Europe and America at that time. Ivan Mazepa was fluent in five languages and was proficient in Latin. A military leader and at the same time a poet, whose poems most tangibly echoed patriotic motives and sympathy for the fate of Ukraine, this hetman held strong appeal for the people of Ukraine. Mazepa struck the hearts of many people because of his diverse skills and interests.

Despite Russia's ban on diplomatic relations with other countries, Mazepa had numerous connections with the monarchical courts of Europe, where he was especially valued. Having learned about the plans of the czar of Russia to eliminate the hetmanate and the Cossack system (which meant the destruction of Ukraine's statehood), Mazepa began secret negotiations with the Swedish and Polish kings to successfully stand up to the czar of Moscow. More than two centuries later, the Russian Orthodox Church still has not revoked Mazepa's excommunication. This is proof that Ivan Mazepa's name and influence upon Ukrainian culture are as alive and prevalent today.

Mazepa, the King of Fire, always stayed true to his values, holding fast to his core beliefs. This king prized culture, creativity, and beauty as the cultural foundation for the people of his country. He reminds us to always watch over and protect what is of utmost importance to us.

---

1. Гетьман translates as hetman and stands for the highest military officer in the hetmanates area of Ukraine, the Zaporizhian Host.

2 OF FIRE

Feeling: Dance of energies, rhythm, movement, collaboration, spirit-inspired action.

Ask yourself: How do I master collaboration and partnership with others so that we can cocreate a masterpiece?

Action: Act on spirit-inspired, communal decisions. Move forward, plan, and execute.

Essence: When we dance our part in harmony with the energy of the universal dance, we contribute to the collective frequency.

NOTES

Dancers circle tightly, holding one another in a ring of celebration and collaboration. Alternating man and woman, this close-knit ring is bound with hands clasped behind the backs of those next to them. The synchronous movements of the Коломийка[1] dancers are full of purpose and energy, moving around and around in a joyful circle. Time halts to take in this spectacle of movement.

Коломийка is a beautiful Ukrainian folk dance that combines folklore, ancient tradition, and music. It is fiery and lyrical, unrestrained and slow, capturing the depth of the human experience. Dancers move in a circle, forming a single "kolo," or sun, which typifies the gathering of people at any celebration. In Ukrainian folk dance, Коломийка is distinguished by the richness of dance movements, the artistry of choreography, and the lively pace of performance, impressing the audience with its bright colors. This dance showcases the fellowship of partnership and the mastery of collaboration between the dancers.

Коломийка is a powerful and eloquent art form that combines poetry, music, and dance. The expressive performance of Коломийка's dances can also be accompanied by bursts of melodious and emphatic singing. The dancers exuberantly sing the chorus, chanting short stanzas, which often hint at the greater meaning of the dance.

Due to the unusual richness and diversity of the Коломийка's language, it is believed that anyone who wants to learn to speak well must learn that dance by heart. And because of their humorous, life-affirming pathos, Коломийка are not forgotten but are passed down from generation to generation.

This vibrant Ukrainian folk dance requires precise and harmonic movements in unison with your partner. The masterpiece of the Коломийка creates a thoughtful collaboration and cocreation. The dance demonstrates the power of creating greatness when we work purposefully in community.

---

1. Коломийка is a Hutsul music genre that combines a fast-paced folk dance and comedic rhymed verses. It originated in the west Ukrainian town of Kolomyia, Ivano-Frankivsk region.

3 OF FIRE

Feeling: Strength, commitment, effort, setting goals, making plans, moving from one state to another.

Ask yourself: Where do I take advantage of the generosity that surrounds me?

Action: Cherish and respect the treasures that are given to you through the hearts of others.

Essence: When we cross the line between playfulness and harm, we cause energetic pain that disrupts harmony.

NOTES

As the beautiful music rises and flows from the vibrating strings of the violin, the musician closes his eyes in concentration and commitment to his creation. The violin is a symbol of admiration, a means of expressing the language of our ancestors' souls, and also an invitation to act on your dreams and desires. If you take the instrument in your hands with love and soul, then it will produce a special sound as a gift of her love.

A Ukrainian legend offers a cautionary tale about love and the dangers of playing with the hearts of others. The story begins with a maiden named Smila, whose beauty attracted many suitors. Smila was young and ignorant to the attention of others, and she often responded to their proposals without care or consideration.

In the same village as Smila lived a handsome young man named Demid, who was famous for playing the violin, inspiring people to open their hearts to love. Demid vied for the attention of Smila, but Smila avoided his advancements. One day, Demid could not stand to wait any longer and directly proposed to Smila.

This cunning girl decided to play a trick on Demid. She told him that if he came to her at midnight and played a beautiful melody on his violin, she would agree to become his wife. That evening, he took his magical instrument and went to play for her at the place she directed him to go. Although he played from his heart, no one responded.

When the door finally opened, Demid was ecstatic, thinking that his beloved was inspired to marry him. Instead, an angry man shouted at him to quiet his playing and leave so he could sleep. It was at that moment that Demid knew that Smila had deceived him. Demid was devastated. His heart broken, he went to the river and threw himself into the water. The next day, villagers found only the violin and knew that Smila had caused this. From that day forward, no man dared to suit her.

In the years that followed, Smila became an outcast and reclusive. It is said that on the night of each full moon, Smila walks along the riverbank and longs for the sound of the violin and the man who once loved her.

The violin is a cherished instrument that offers the gift of music. This gift should not be taken lightly, nor should any gift of passion. Do not take advantage of the offerings of others but accept them with purity of heart.

4 OF FIRE

Feeling: Accomplishment, supreme power, dignity, undeniable faith, justice.

Ask yourself: Do I allow myself space to celebrate my achievements in life?

Action: Take time to rest and rejuvenate. Connect with those who helped you, and enjoy the harmony of creation.

Essence: When we honor the balance between determination and rest, we can find enjoyment both in our efforts and our accomplishments.

NOTES

Shining and bold, the mace is solitary against a darkened backdrop, majestic and powerful. This handcrafted tool is well adorned with precious metals and gemstones as a display of supreme power. The wooden handle is topped with a heavy ball called "the apple," then covered in gold or silver with inlaid turquoise, emerald, and pearls. This ancient weapon is both beautiful and deadly, having been used by the hetman[1] of Ukraine and depicting the owner's coat of arms, surname, and monogram. The mace was also seen as a representation of strong will, desire for freedom, courage, and faithfulness to one's word.

According to tradition, the presidential mace has sixty-four stones of emeralds and garnets set in a complex gold setting. Hidden in the mace is a three-sided damask blade with the Latin motto "Omnia revertutur," which translates as "Everything returns," engraved in gilt. These words are significant to the Ukrainian people because of their strong belief in dignity and justice.

The mace, as a symbol of the highest power, was always in a prominent place. For example, during negotiations with the Poles in Lviv, Bohdan Khmelnytskyi[2] sat at the table with a gilded mace. We can see the mace not only as holding artistic value but also carrying a historical significance of power.

The mace offers us a strong reminder that what we reap, so shall we sow. This stunning and significant symbol represents strong foundations for our goals and dreams. The beauty and pride associated with the mace is a reminder of our own internal power and how we can call upon it as a source of unwavering strength into which we can always anchor.

---

1. Гетьман translates as hetman and stands for the highest military officer in the hetmanates area of Ukraine, the Zaporizhian Host.
2. Bohdan Khmelnytskyi—King of Earth

5 OF FIRE

Feeling: The path to ambition is not easy. There are obstacles, even setbacks.

Ask yourself: How do I honor and accept difficulties I come upon in my life?

Action: Look beyond your reality. This will free you to accept barriers in your life as unforeseen opportunities.

Essence: When we are willing to open our hearts to see that life's challenges are blessings, they bring us nearer to manifesting opulence in this lifetime.

NOTES

Sparks fly as the blacksmith wields his hammer with strength and grace. Using his forge and anvil, he transmutes the once-cold and firm iron into artifacts of service. Bestowed with Svarog's[1] skills, the blacksmith loses himself in the craft of creating, with a divine combination of heat and force. The image of the mighty blacksmith's strength is equally matched with his creativity, offering us a glimpse into true divine masculinity.

Blacksmiths were treated with great respect and admiration as benevolent wizards, possessing the complex and mysterious art of transforming metal into tools, both beautiful and useful. It was clear that this form of fine craftsmanship of such masterpieces could not be derived simply from materials and experience. Those who dealt with iron and fire were perceived as servants under the protection of Svarog, the heavenly god of the blacksmith, who is believed to have forged the universe. As such, blacksmithing has always been inextricably linked with magic. Everything created by the blacksmith was considered magical, from mighty weapons to common practical items such as utensils, tools, and jewelry.

Blacksmiths were also seen as protectors from evil forces. The horseshoe, the blacksmith's primary product, had practical uses but was also seen as a conduit and container for universal energy. The blacksmith that forged these magical items was held in high regard, and the foundry in which he worked was usually viewed as a safe place for men to meet and share the gifts of brotherhood.

The blacksmith understands how we are forged in fire and how intense heat and pressure can create the outcomes we seek. He is a powerful reminder of how we can discover newfound gifts and blessings in any of our challenges, obstacles, or setbacks that we come upon in our lifetime.

---

1. Svarog—Major Arcana #4

6 OF FIRE

Feeling: Recognition of efforts, success, achievements, courage, freedom.

Ask yourself: How can I use my experiences to illuminate the path for others?

Action: Be comfortable in stepping forward into your light, and share your wisdom generously with others.

Essence: When we share personally, with the best interests of others at heart, it allows them to find happiness and brings us together in collective celebration.

NOTES

Ripe red berries hang from the lush viburnum tree, absorbing and reflecting the warm and nourishing light of the sun. Basking in autumn's light, the viburnum leaves are laden with the amber glow of the fruit of Ukraine. The richness of this sacred plant foretells the love and happiness of the hearth and home.

Since the viburnum berries are red in color, they became associated with blood, life, and immortality. The fruits of viburnum became a symbol of the steadfastness of spirit and the connection to the homeland of Ukraine. Every home was built with a viburnum bush in the yard as a strong foundation for the home and family.

The viburnum holds tremendous meaning for women, since it is a symbol of her whole spiritual life: her girlhood, beauty and love, marriage, joy and sorrow, and devotion to family.

A legend told to children involved the love of two sisters. They both fell in love with the same handsome suitor, and neither would relinquish their claim for his love. The young man was forced to choose, and he knew that his heart was with the younger sister. The elder daughter could see the passion between the man and her sibling, so the elder sister took the life of her sister and buried her in a field. As time passed, a viburnum bush sprouted and grew strong and healthy over the young maid's grave. The young man, still grieving, was drawn to the tree and used one of its branches to fashion a flute. As he played the flute, he could hear the voice of his beloved in the melody, telling the story of her demise, but also reminding him of her love for him. The man was able to live with solace, knowing that she had not abandoned their union and that she truly loved him.

The viburnum is a powerful plant, whose medicine helps us recognize truth, connection, and familial prosperity. It embodies the light of the sun and helps illuminate our path and that of others, through our God-given wisdom. Through our boundless actions, the viburnum reminds us to share our truths and to encourage others to embody the same qualities so that they can realize the same happiness.

7 OF FIRE

Feeling: Jumping high to achieve goals, getting on top of things.

Ask yourself: What is possible if I am willing to commit with absolute faith and trust?

Action: Illuminate your inner light and follow the path that is lit up before you.

Essence: When we choose the path that is our heart's calling, the universe opens in parallel, revealing to us all its possibilities.

NOTES

On the shortest night of the year, glowing bonfires burn across the lands, radiating heat and throwing their light upward into the blackness. While the sun rests for its longest slumber, brave young Ukrainians take a leap of faith over the flames, to cleanse and protect themselves of the evil that accompanies this night. The spirit of Ivana Kupala's night[1] is ablaze, and fear is quelled as they pass over the flame and through the glittering sparks of this night's fire.

Every year, on the night of the summer solstice, the fate of the world was decided, and the light of hope has always prevailed over evil darkness. However, the forces of light were never solitary in their struggle against the dark. As dark descends on this special night, many brave young souls partake in traditions to help illuminate the world to ward off evil. Before lighting a fire, four men with torches become a square around a bush, denoting the four seasons. Then friends, companions, and community come forth to light a chosen bush aflame in the forest. The fire is always lit after sunset and is kept burning until after dawn.

Individuals take part in this jubilant ritual for the benefit both of themselves and the rest of the world. If you jump over the Kupala's fire on this night, your soul will be cleansed and you will become healthier and happier, free of all negativity and diseases. The higher you leap over the flames, the more good fortune and luck would come to you.

For couples who take part in the ceremony, it is important to know that you cannot jump over the Kupala bonfire with just anyone, but only hand in hand with your soulmate. As the couple leaps over the fire, if their hands do not part, they will have a strong and happy marriage in the future. When you do so, the magic fire reveals a future of happiness to the partners.

Jumping over the Ivana Kupala bonfire takes trust and reassurance, knowing that the outcome will most certainly be beautiful and rewarding. Traditions remind us that we cannot ever take this leap without absolute commitment and faith in the power of goodness, hope, and light. Great things are awaiting us all.

---

1. Night of Ivana Kupala—10 of Fire

8 OF FIRE

Feeling: Strength, power, loyalty, bravery, great hustle, hope, and a final trust toward the end of the project.

Ask yourself: How can I make room in my heart for more joy?

Action: Practice daily gratitude for where you are at in the present moment.

Essence: When we stay humble and grateful, we create a momentum to celebrate the positive changes and transformation in life.

NOTES

Between the worlds of the living and the dead resides a harmonious intermediary, the horse. From ancient times, the horse is known to have been blessed with a gift of prophecy and can even hear death, a wedded union, or the arrival of spring, twelve days in advance. Because of his place in this world and his abilities, he is often called upon as a loyal helper by gods and heroes.

The horse is an assistant and soothsayer that can perform miracles. In children's fairy tales, the grandmother would always describe the horse as someone who could make a hero handsome or turn him into the most royal of palaces. There are legends of how these strong, heroic horses not only could outlast a dozen men but could also fly "higher than standing forests." As they soar high through the sky, they will seek out their rightful owner, who lives an ordinary life and does not yet suspect he is a hero. Only when his time has arrived can the yet-unrecognized hero take stride upon his steed and go "to the border" to guard against snakes.[1]

The horse has always been revered in Ukrainian folklore as an animal of vast strength, attuned senses, and eternal loyalty. He remains to this day as a reliable and wise companion to the hero, man, the Cossack.[2]

---

1. Snake—8 of Water
2. Cossack—Major Arcana #8

9 OF FIRE

Feeling: Searching for the true path, seeking help, illuminating all sides and aspects of the situation, a feeling of "battered but not defeated."

Ask yourself: How often do I rush into making a decision without making sure I have the right support?

Action: Bring more clarity to the situation; be patient with the timing.

Essence: When we illuminate the path before starting to walk it, it saves us from unnecessary onslaughts, blocks, and U-turns.

NOTES

Spásivka is full of abundance and bounty. Handwoven baskets, adorned with poppies and wildflowers, are filled with brightly colored blossoms, young fruits, and sweet honey. The basket of early-harvest fruits and flowers is not only a gift from the Mother Earth, but a welcome sign of hope for an even-larger fall harvest.

Since ancient times, we call the beginning of August Spásivka, the First Harvest. It is a time when the spirits and souls of our ancestors appear on Earth, to visit their families and support the rituals of blessing Mother Earth's new gifts. Spásivka celebrations bless the home and harvest, to guarantee the abundance of everything until the next year. Ancestors and spirits come to contribute to the flowering and ripening of fruits and to the protection of the fields, orchards, and gardens. This is why Ukrainian people believe that the first vegetables, flowers, honeycombs, and bread from the August harvest hold special potency and ancestral wisdom.

In Ukraine, the magic of the beginning is revered. Therefore, on these days, people prepare the festive baskets for consecration. As per tradition, festive baskets contain freshly ripe apples, plums, pears, and honey.

Various flowers are added for specific blessings to the home and family. Wormwood serves as a talisman against all kinds of misfortune. Cornflower offers peace to the whole family. Curlews encourage boys to look after the girls. Nightshades encompass a celestial body that is supposed to be merciful to all living things. The composition is adorned with twigs of viburnum, which symbolize female happiness, and oats, which embody the immeasurable harvest and wealth. Poppies are particularly potent and powerful and are sprinkled in the home to ward off evil spirits.

Spásivka, or the First Harvest, is a time of hope and patience. This card reminds us to ask for and accept help from our ancestors and guides. Careful plans and consistent actions are necessary for our desired results. While we may feel fatigued by sowing seeds and tending our garden of dreams, trust and timing will bring bountiful harvest.

10 OF FIRE

Feeling: Mystery, magic, burning away what no longer serves, duality, fight of opposites.

Ask yourself: What is stopping me from taking action and moving forward with my dreams?

Action: Cleanse yourself from any foreign entities and attachments that are holding you back. Do not take on any new commitments. Say a firm no to things that do not serve you.

Essence: When the fire within us is lit, it lights up everyone around you. Keep it alive!

NOTES

Flames burn high and bright on the night of Ivana Kupala,[1] sending sparks like wishes into the dark sky. Black silhouettes in the distance hold untold stories of evil spirits and demons, but near the fire, celebration is all that matters. Youthful dancers circle the great flames, to honor the god of the highest sun.

In Ukraine, the holiday of Ivana Kupala symbolizes the connection between man and nature and the transition to the summer cycle of pre-Christian calendar holidays.

Our ancestors believed that witches and evil spirits come to Earth on this night, and water and fire protect them. There are two purification rites that can be chosen: water or fire. The ancestors believed that it was necessary to swim in open water on this night, to help cleanse the body and soul of bad thoughts and evil. The healing properties of the water are both curative and purifying. Washing the body with water brought beauty to women and strength to men. There is a legend that on the day of Ivana Kupala, the early-morning dew holds life-giving and rejuvenating properties, so it is recommended to walk barefoot on the grass.

There are also Kupala fire purification rituals. On the night of Ivana Kupala, our ancestors gathered around the fire, which bore a wheel on a high pole as a symbol of the sun. Young people danced around the sacred fire, eventually joining hands with their partner to jump over the flames. This was a test to see if the couple were soulmates. If their hands remained joined, they would stay happy together forever.

In the eighteenth century a number of documents appeared, testifying to the fierce struggle of the church with the Kupala rite. In 1719, there was a law that gave the right to physically punish and excommunicate all the participants of the Kupala games. Then, in 1723, the church banned dancing and celebrating near the Kupala bonfire. Later, Catherine II issued a decree banning the holiday completely. Despite all prohibitions, the beautiful celebration of Light stayed in the hearts of our ancestors and was secretly held in distant fields and forests. Ivana Kupala is still celebrated by Ukrainians around the world.

Ivana Kupala is a night filled with magic and ritual, manifestation and celebration. This night reminds us to release that which does not serve and to embrace our grandest dreams. Build a community to support you, and release attachments that keep you from living your best life.

---

1. Night of Ivana Kupala—Ace of Fire

MINOR ARCANA
EARTH

Ace of Earth

Feeling: Unconditional love and eternal support. Wisdom, prophecy, mother's love, new beginnings on a material level, opportunity for prosperity.

Ask yourself: What is wanting to be birthed through my life experiences on this earth?

Action: Take conscious action; you influence the web of life and creation.

Essence: When we are aligned with our higher calling, we can manifest abundance and prosperity by weaving the thread of plenty and limitless generosity.

Notes

The goddess Mokosha draws us into the warmth of her bosom, as she blesses all living things. The lush greenery is lovingly nourished by Mokosha, Great Mother Earth, since she is the bearer of all life. Her gentle demeanor is reflected in her kind and maternal visage as she illuminates all with her beauty and kindness.

Mokosha is considered the Mother of all living creatures and plants, the center of fertility. She creates beginnings in life and uses her discretion to initiate endings. According to the Slavic tradition, the earth is a symbol of motherhood and femininity. It is believed that thunder wakes her up in the spring. Taking in the seed, Mokosha becomes pregnant and gives a new crop. She is the universal Mother and Nurturer, who feeds the living and returns the dead into the cycle. She is the one who gives birth to everything.

The goddess Mokosha is the patroness of women and girls. She takes care of fertility, women's needlework, housekeeping, marriage, childbirth, and prosperity in the home. This midwife is the great guardian of the holy spirit of the ancestors, who gives birth to a new life for happiness, with faith and hope for a better destiny.

From the beginning, people have long honored the great goddess Mokosha during harvest festivals, since she is the Great Mother Earth. Her name literally translates as "Mother of a Full Basket," mother of abundance. Mokosha is associated with the female sphere in the economy, which includes needlework, spinning, weaving, and sewing. Mokosha spins the Fortune's Wheel[1] and weaves in the good fate for humanity. That is why the worship of Mokosha lingered the longest among women.

Mokosha reminds us of our unconditional love for Mother Earth. She brings nourishment, care, and abundance. All of life is given care and support though the Great Mother, reminding us of our connection to all life.

---

1. Fortune's Wheel—Major Arcana #10

Page of Earth

Feeling: Gentle beginnings in the material world, establishing a foundation for future endeavors, news about a new commitment.

Ask yourself: How do I move forward with integrity so that my legacy perseveres to serve humanity?

Action: Start the project or idea you have been dreaming of. You have the support you require to realize the success of this endeavor.

Essence: When we ground our dreams in reality and gently move through life, we inspire others to take the initial steps toward achieving their own dreams.

Notes

Precious pastel bells surround the tall and sturdy stalk of the mallow flower. Its pale colorful hues decorate the gardens, homes, and hillsides of Ukraine, delighting in the adoration of those who behold her beauty.

In Ukrainian folk culture, the mallow flower, or malva, is the keeper of the Ukrainian home, a symbol of our motherland and our spiritual heritage. She is a symbol of love for country, her people, and her father's house. The mallow represents wisdom, faith, hope, and love.

This flower is among the most common in Ukraine. A fond childhood memory of Ukrainians is the tall pastel-colored flowers that grew near the house or in the countryside. Manors were decorated with them, and there was not a village, home, or flower garden where mallows—talismans of spiritual heritage—did not grow near the mud or under the windows.

A legend tells of a brave and fearless girl named Malva who loved her native land and its people. It was a long time ago when the Turks and Tatars would rob our lands and take Ukrainian people as slaves. Only the beautiful young girl Malva stood up against the raiders. She would not consent to leave her native land, and so she fought valiantly to protect her village and motherland. Her captors would not relent and struck the girl with their weapons. As Malva fought, her blood fell in droplets to the earth, and after a time she finally succumbed. Although the brave girl died in her fight for freedom, her legend was remembered. The following spring, on each spot where Malva had bled, beautiful flowers bloomed. From that time forward, the people called this flower malva in honor of the most sacred of things—the love for one's home and native land.

The mallow flower is grounding and sturdy, giving us courage to live in alignment with your values. It is a reminder that you have purpose, no matter how small you may feel. With inner strength, your aspirations will be realized, and then its goodness will ripple out into the wider world.

MESSENGER OF EARTH

Feeling: Rebirth, transformation, and prophecy. Energy of healing and nurturing.

Ask yourself: Can I discern what my truth is, so I can let go of things that do not serve me? How can I create meaningful results for my future, starting now?

Action: Listen with all your senses, both physical and psychic, to the messages you receive from the world around you.

Essence: When we are aligned, determined, and dedicated, our effort over time proves to be prosperous and rewarding.

NOTES

The cuckoo is crowned and is considered a queen among its peers. Perched high on a pine bough, she can see farther than we can imagine. Her dark shining eyes, like drops of obsidian, have the power to glance into the future and heal the past. With the gift of prophecy and truth, the cuckoo signifies growth, healing, and rebirth.

The cuckoo is seen as an established and indisputable symbol of omniscience. Often, people would ask the cuckoo to foretell the future. As a messenger of both life and death, she could tell you how many more years you would live, or predict future health and prosperity.

The cuckoo is a pronounced feminine image, carrying marriage symbolism, often seen in decorative embroidery. In spite of her matriarchal associations, it is said that the cuckoo is so busy with the demands of her fortune-telling that she does not have time to hatch her eggs into chicks. Once she lays her eggs, the cuckoo hides them in the nest of another bird so that her babies will have a warm, loving mother to look after them.

However, the cuckoo holds much more mystery than as a childless widow. It was believed that she could also take our sorrows away forever. Women would often craft a figurine of the bird with sticks and cloth. They would solemnly bring the cuckoo with them into the woods, where they would leave her. As they parted, they would whisper to the cuckoo, asking for her to carry away their sorrows and grief.

The cuckoo is an intuitive and visionary being. She reminds us that all we wish for is waiting for and available to us. We just need to remain open to hearing the messages from the physical and psychic world. Then, we can proceed to create the desired change we seek through living a life of kindness and compassion.

Queen of Earth

Feeling: Resourceful, rigorous, fair, and grounded. An effective and intelligent communicator, earthy. A very responsible person, who knows how to balance life with justice and mercy.

Ask yourself: Can I act with ferocity when it is called upon to do what is right?

Action: Act boldly with resolve to do what is necessary to move forward.

Essence: When we take steadfast measures, we find clarity of conscience.

Notes

Княгиня[1] Olga became famous far beyond the homeland for her wisdom and iron character. This outstanding historical figure was a wise, strong, charismatic woman who became the ruler of Kyivan Rus after the death of her husband, Князь Ігор.[2] Olga's extraordinary personal qualities ensured that she did not falter after Князь Ігор's passing, as she took the reins of power to guide her country.

Olga, with her brutality, managed to streamline the tax collection system (for the imperfection of which, in fact, her husband was killed), to create the first strongholds of Kyiv authorities, which actually became the first administrative and territorial elements in Kyivan Rus.

In foreign policy, the support of Byzantium was extremely important for Kyivan Rus, so Olga approached Constantine, who was emperor at the time. According to the legend, he fell in love with the princess and wished to take her as his wife, and at the same time the great state of Kyivan Rus. She found an opportunity in this. Since Olga wanted to adopt Christianity as a religion, she resorted to trickery to outsmart the emperor. Olga asked Constantine to personally baptize her, since she could not marry him due to the fact she was pagan. Once baptized, Olga declared to Constantine that she still could not marry him, since marrying a godfather was considered to be a great sin. Having understood the ruse, Constantin let the princess go but remained her ardent admirer thereafter.

Olga's conversion to Christianity had a huge impact on the acceptance of the religion in Europe, since she was an ardent agent of change and a catalyst in ensuring that the religion was spread far and wide.

Княгиня Olga exemplified the perfect blend of characteristics as a ruler: wisdom and determination, justice and rigor, firmness and mercy, perseverance and kindness. All these traits lent themselves toward helping her to successfully rule the largest state in Europe, without any wars, for approximately twenty years. This is a record for any ancient Kyivan Rus ruler but is especially exceptional since she was a woman. Before Olga, women had never ruled in the land of Ukraine, nor have they since her time.

---

1. Княгиня is a historical Slavic title, used both as a royal and noble title, and is usually translated into English as princess or duchess.

2. Князь Ігор: grand duke of Kyivan Rus, the Rurik dynasty.

King of Earth

Feeling: Grounded, iron will, strong, practical, valor, fearless, courageous advocate, command, reliable leader.

Ask yourself: How do I create a disciplined routine to attract abundance in my life?

Action: Proceed with deliberate and firm habits, despite oncoming constraints.

Essence: Humbleness, groundedness, and tenacity are readily available to us as the simplest pathway to completion.

Notes

Bohdan Khmelnytsky was a reformer and founder of Ukrainian statehood who led with fearless strength of purpose and bold determination to influence others and bring about independence for his country. It was he who gave the term "Ukraine" a political influence as a state.

The roots of the Ukrainian nation as an ethnic entity date back to the time of Khmelnytsky. At the political level, we began to be called Ukraine, and our people Ukrainians. Bohdan was a prominent diplomat and a skillful, experienced politician. Under his rulership, Ukraine was acknowledged as a formal state and subsequently firmly established itself at the international level. Khmelnytsky created unified government structures that worked purely in the best interests of the Ukrainian state. These were their own armed forces; customs, financial, postal, and judicial services; and internal and external trade.

As Гетьман Війська Запорозького,[1] Bohdan was unwavering in his march toward his goal of standing up for the will and independence of the Ukrainian people and their land. He was a national hero who brought great honor and glory to Ukrainian history, since he was the first to stand up for the will and independence of the Ukrainian people and their native land.

Гетьман Bohdan Khmelnytsky always worked with careful planning, strictness, diligence, and bold action in achieving his goals. He never settled for anything less than his grandest desire for the successes of his country. The ambitious will, energy, and character of this hetman was manifested in many life situations. Yet, even after occupying a high-ranking position, Khmelnytsky led a simple soldier's life, showing moderation in his personal life.

---

1. Гетьман Війська Запорозького: The head of state of the Ukrainian Cossack State.

2 OF EARTH

Feeling: Divine connection, eternal legacy, immortality of our human's soul.

Ask yourself: How do my actions impact those around me now?

Action: Expand your awareness and consider how your choices will affect future generations.

Essence: When we take pride and ownership in what we do in this lifetime, we create a persistent pattern of good intention for the next generations across lifetimes.

NOTES

We often call Дідух[1] the Great-Grandfather, since he is not only the symbol of harvest, but also the representation of an immortal ancestor—the founder of the family, the spiritual life of Ukrainians, and a talisman of the family. Дідух is the connection between our generations that must persist forever unbroken. It is a symbol of wealth, well-being, peace, and life.

Дідух is represented in the binding of the last sheaf of grain from the year's harvest. The ears of the sheaf, bound from wheat, rye, oats, or all together, were adorned with colored ribbons, dried wildflowers, and viburnum branches. It was believed that this sheaf contained all the life-giving power of the harvest, and, once arranged, it was brought from the field and then carefully put aside for safekeeping. Only on the evening of winter solstice is it brought, with great honor, into the house and placed on a bench for reverence, where it will spend the season.

During the Great-Grandfather's stay in the house, the souls of all of our relatives come together. The tradition of placing a Дідух on the table of the Holy Supper is rooted into the heart of our nation, since he himself is everything that Ukrainians value most—family connection, connection with our ancestors, and connection with our native land.

Дідух is a time-honored tradition that dates back to pre-Christian times as one of the oldest Christmas rituals of Ukrainians. The Great-Grandfather is an annual reminder of our immortal ancestor and the forever-binding bond between the generations.

---

1. Дідух: Didukh literally means "grandfather spirit." Didukh is traditionally made from the first or the last stalks of wheat reaped during the harvest season.

3 OF EARTH

Feeling: Invisible power, nobility, creating a new source of income, setting up a foundation for the future, dedication, love for your vocation.

Ask yourself: Is what you do aligned with your heart calling? Does it bring you joy and serve your higher purpose?

Action: Step back and reassess what is completed at this initial stage of the journey.

Essence: When we proceed with what is called from our heart, we become both the conduit and the cocreator of Spirit's will on this Earth.

NOTES

The kobza's loom is huge and majestic in the embrace of its player. As the musician plays, the magic emanates the ether with music and story. The player's grace belies her strength and purpose, for she knows the power of her melody.

The kobza is one of the oldest Ukrainian folk string instruments of the lute family. It is usually made of willow or linden wood, giving it a special rhythm, a connected performance style, and a deep emotional and spiritual relationship with our people.

The music of the kobza is the voice of thousands of years and the spirit of the ancestors, which resounds through the ages in the form of hundreds of thousands of songs, chants, carols, and hymns.

The kobza is often named one of the original creations of the Ukrainian people, which began to spread widely from the end of the sixteenth century. It is a symbolic instrument for Ukraine and was a favorite instrument of the Cossacks.[1]

Those who played the kobza were known as Kobzars.[2] They were officially part of the Zaporizhzhya army and performed Cossack military music with drummers and trumpeters. Later, these musicians traveled through the cities and villages of Ukraine, singing freedom-loving poems and historical songs in which they glorified the exploits of brave Cossacks and called for a fight against oppressors. The melody of the kobza is one of bravery, history, and courage of our nation. Because of this, the musicians were often persecuted as enemies of those who could not tolerate the Ukrainian traditions.

The history of the kobza has gradually evolved, gaining fame, power, and magic. Like this beautiful instrument, we are tied both to the past and the future; our lives are the conduit of music and expression. Listen to your heart and share its story, as a message from Spirit, here on Earth.

---

1. Cossack—Major Arcana #8
2. Kobzar—Major Arcana #12

4 OF EARTH

Feeling: Freedom, courage, independence, endurance.

Ask yourself: How can I lay out a solid foundation to move forward with my goals?

Action: Seek out clarity and focus precisely on what is a priority for you.

Essence: When we create with coherence, the whole universe will provide the support in this endeavor.

NOTES

There is a particular luminous glow surrounding the trident, an image found on the Ukraine Coat of Arms. It is one of the three officially recognized symbols of Ukraine, in addition to the flag[1] and anthem.[2] The trident is both regal and imposing, and its three symmetrical points convey faith, strength, and independence.

This trinity, which is significant in the meaning of the trident, has accompanied humanity since the birth of the first civilizations. These are always three equal forces originating from the Absolute, which is inherent in every culture.

According to our ancestors' beliefs, the trident represents the origin, which personifies the trinity of the feminine (Mokosha,[3] the left part), the masculine (Dashbog, the right part), and the deity who takes care of life and death (Marena,[4] in the center).

Since the trident is such a long-standing and powerful symbol, there are innumerable interpretations of it in the Ukrainian culture. Some interpretations include an ancient religious sign, a falcon, an anchor, an ear of rye, a bow with an arrow, a crown, a triune sacrifice in the name of the victory of life over death, and the tip of a Byzantine or Scythian scepter of the king.

The trident presents our country as a sovereign, independent state and is an official emblem depicted on official documents, seals, and money. Its oldest images on coins, dishes, and seals that were used to seal international treaties were found by archeologists and date back to the tenth century.

On February 19, 1992, the Parliament of Ukraine, by its resolution, approved the State Coat of Arms of independent Ukraine. It became a golden trident on a blue shield, a sign of the Kyiv state during the reign of Volodymyr the Great, which symbolizes the continuity of the long historical development of the Ukrainian people. An olive wreath was depicted around the symbol as a sign of peace.

---

1. Flag—4 of Air
2. Anthem—4 of Water
3. Mokosha—Ace of Earth
4. Marena—Major Arcana #13

5 OF EARTH

Feeling: Overlooked treasures, hardship, worry over money, financial challenges, sacred craft, the illusion of abundance or lack.

Ask yourself: How can I shift my perspective from one of poverty to prosperity?

Action: Pause and take account of the gifts and blessings, many of which may be unseen to you.

Essence: Energy flows where the focus goes. When we consciously see life with a lens of graciousness and gratitude, we can see that we have already received the universe's flow of constant abundance.

NOTES

The early-morning sun shines upon the smiling face of the bread maker as she pours her love into the dough she is kneading together with gifts of generosity and abundance from nature. This traditional work of art is crafted from the very fruit of the sun, called Колосок.[1] The bread maker is able to provide blessings of nutrition and sustenance only with an open humble heart, knowing that her work is a finished product of many hands that bring the nourishing grains from harvest to table.

Bread making is vital to the life of the Ukrainian people. Bread is sacred to our people and has become a defining symbol of spiritual wealth of the Ukrainian people, grown with their own hands on their God-given, native land. Ukrainian bakers believed that there is no tastier bread than the one you bake yourself. So each housewife keeps her special recipe for making bread a secret, perfecting it and passing it on to the next generation.

Embodied in the grains of each loaf is the energy of sun and the earth that connects each of us to our divine Father and Mother. Through association, the one who grows the grains is a son of the sun—a divine and holy man. Farmers partake in the ritual of plowing, fieldwork, and harvesting in such a way that they infuse love and respect into their work. Many rites and traditions were associated with the work of farmers, the most sacred of which is bread making.

The tradition of wheat farming and bread making have contributed to the unity of the Ukrainian people and their spiritual enrichment. Sun worshipers, bread workers, and bread makers live in harmony with nature and understand their dependence on natural cycles, and therefore their way of thinking and rhythm of life is determined by Mother Nature and her natural cycles.

In recognition of the sacredness of wheat, we value both the farmers and the tradition of bread making, bringing together the sun and earth elements. These revered artisans are creators of bounty, from nothing more than a small seed. They remind us to look again at our situation, to recognize and cherish the gifts that abound.

---

1. Колосок: An ear of grain or wheat.

6 OF EARTH

Feeling: Strength, morale, resilience, and knowledge. A powerful combination of wise rulership and generosity.

Ask yourself: How can I openly come forward and seek guidance and assistance without fear of seeming weak or powerless?

Action: Be willing to ask for help when you need it with sincerity and honesty.

Essence: When we are able to earnestly ask for support, the universe is always ready to provide generosity and abundance.

NOTES

The oak is a strong and stable tree, with power and rigidity but also with beauty and grace. The steadfast and reliable oak stands alone, anchored firmly in the soil, reaching upward toward the sun as a majestic pillar brimming with masculine life force.

The oak bravely stands after every storm. His stability comes from the expansive far-reaching roots, providing solidity to the ground underlying the surrounding foliage. Emerald leaves decorate his bold limbs, while rich sunbeams cast shadows around the solid trunk, providing cooling shade for plants and animals that seek respite from the sun's warm rays. The oak also provides protection for small animals that live within his hollowed caverns, further demonstrating how he lives in harmonious coexistence with his environment.

Once an oak grows and is fully rooted, he stands resolutely for his beliefs and goals. By its nature, he never bends—the oak can only be broken! There is nothing he cannot achieve.

In Ukrainian mythology, the oak was called the Svarog[1] tree—the god of masculine energy and the developer of life. In songs, the image of the oak is understood as a man, a young Cossack,[2] strong and brave and unmoving in its mandate of protection. More than once, the oak has been a place of sacred rites, initiations, and rituals, so it is understandable that this powerful tree is associated with and symbolizes good health, longevity, and prosperity.

From time immemorial and across all of the world's continents, the wise oak has been a silent witness to our history. It is a constant reminder that we all are strong and that our past ancestors are always watching over and providing for us.

---

1. Svarog—Major Arcana #4
2. Cossack—Major Arcana #8

7 OF EARTH

Feeling: Rejection, need to change plans, seeking wisdom in relationships, including business and money.

Ask yourself: What lesson did I learn from these past events?

Action: Reassess your past efforts and start again. Continue by choosing a different path. Look for new strategies or alternative routes.

Essence: There is no right or wrong, good or bad. When we make decisions based on the fact that all events are simply neutral, we can then proceed with integrity and grace.

NOTES

A beautiful girl holds a ripe pumpkin at the threshold of her home, as part of the Ukrainian matchmaking tradition. She lingers near the door, unwilling to leave, and yet, looking longingly out into the wider world. Yes, she is lovely and ready to meet her mate, but perhaps this particular one is not "the One." The pumpkin, nourishing and whole, is a token gift to her rejected suitor, reminding him that there is something good to be gained at each closing door.

The wedding was always preceded by the matchmaking ceremony. The most-respected elders in the village, with "a hanging tongue" or "the gift of gab," were chosen to set out to find a suitable match for the young man. The fate of the wedding actually depended on the eloquence of the matchmakers. If the girl was an enviable bride and had many suitors, then matchmaking played almost the main role here. Experienced matchmakers could convince the girl's parents and the young woman herself that the prospective groom was the best for her future happiness and abundance. Ukrainian embroidered towels were given to the elders, tied over their shoulders, if an agreement was reached at the betrothal. If the girl did not want to get married, then, with the approval of her parents, she brought the boy a pumpkin. The skill of the matchmaker would determine whether the groom would leave with a wedding towel or a pumpkin.

According to the history of our land, the pumpkin, as the symbol of rejection, was motivated by the natural properties of the pumpkin. The people have long known the soothing effect of the gourd on the human body. Ukrainians believed that dishes made from the fruits of this common garden plant could ease stress and emotional pain. In times long ago, after a failed courtship, when the young man ate the pumpkin, his interest in the girl disappeared. This tradition was never offensive, but tactful and wise.

The pumpkin is a symbol of the failure of a potential relationship or match. While it may feel painful at first, rejection of a proposal or partnership is not always a bad thing. Sometimes, "no" is the best answer to receive. Look for the lessons, reassess your choices, and start again.

8 OF EARTH

Feeling: Hard work that brings joy and results in prosperity, actively engaged in life, employment, craftsmanship, commission.

Ask yourself: How will today's efforts result in building wealth in my life?

Action: Support yourself as you are moving forward and working on obtaining new skills in business and life. Express gratitude to your body and mind as it works perfectly to sustain you through the new learning.

Essence: When we create a new level of wisdom with diligence and heart, the committed work is rewarded.

NOTES

The bee lies gently in the center of the blossom, dusted in rich golden pollen, spreading joy and gratitude to those who gaze upon it. This tiny yet capable flier works tirelessly, harvesting nature's goodness while simultaneously pollinating the flowers that grow. The honey that comes from the bees' toil is sweet and life-giving, with properties to please both kings and gods. What a treasure is this mystical little creature, full of ambition and purpose!

The bee was believed to be a sacred creature, winged messenger of the gods, and harbinger of the future. The bee belongs to the pure and divine creatures and is highly respected among people. She brings many messages and holds multiple meanings. On one hand, she is the Holy Worker of God, a symbol of wisdom, diligence, and frugality, associated with the sun. On the other hand, many believe that the bee is the soul of a dead person, due to her sacred essence; it has long been considered sacrilegious and a bad omen to kill her.

Honey produced by the bee is symbolic of prosperity, diligence, and work ethic. Since our culture views bees as messengers of the gods, their honey has also been compared to the nectar of the gods, thus elevating bees to the status of royalty.

Bees have long been mystical messengers in Ukrainian folklore. According to ancient legends, if a bee sits on your hand, you will receive money. If the bee sits on your head, you will achieve great heights in life. Many believe that to see the bee in a dream foretells profit for one's business. If the bees leave the hive for no apparent reason, this is a sure sign of the host's impending death. And if the bee swarm sits on a dry branch of a fruit tree, this is an indication of the death of the owner of the tree or any person who had the misfortune to pass under the swarm.

The bee brings a message of prosperity and success. She reminds us that hard work and diligence are the foundations for forward movement, while joy and gratitude are the tools for fulfillment and success. Heart-centered work always pays off.

9 OF EARTH

Feeling: Material success, prudence, accomplishment, prosperity, independent wealth, concrete results, fortune, treasures.

Ask yourself: How do I honor the land and lineage I was born into?

Action: Use gratitude daily as a deep energetic cord to amplify the connection of what is already abundant in your life.

Essence: When we live aligned with our traditions and honor our heritage, we invoke even more powers to allow abundance to flow through us.

NOTES

The stone oven is sacred to the home and family and is depicted on the colorful hearthstones surrounding it. In Ukraine, the hearth is a central part of the home and is adorned with festive tiles representing the rich Ukrainian culture and all the blessings of the land. These hearthstones are decorated with beautiful folk images to show gratitude for the prosperity and abundance in the home and family.

The stone oven is a symbol of the spiritual bearing of the fruit, the integrity of the family, and the continuity of life. The fire in the oven was considered sacred, so the hostess treated it gently, with respect. Such sanctity was embedded into the genetic memory of the family. Such reverence will always bring us back to the good fire in the hearth of the family house, near which entire generations of our ancestors were born and grew up.

The stove oven in the house is like a mother in the family. The Ukrainian oven fed, warmed, and treated the people in the home and served as a reminder to come back into spiritual alignment so they could live in unity. The moment the fire was lit in the fireplace, it became the center of the home, to which everyone gravitated.

The stove oven is primarily a hearth. It played the role not only of a tool for warmth in the home, but also a spiritual and unifying altar. Historically, the hearth was a symbol of the family's strength, its rallying point and shrine. Since the stove was viewed as a living patroness, our ancestors had a special practice of decorating it with handmade clay bricks. Tiles were always handmade from clay found in local quarries, with the intention that the land would hold the fire and the elements would serve to protect the house and family with its magic.

The stove oven carries the strength of spiritual beliefs and the practicality of daily tasks. When we live our lives in alignment with our traditions and spiritual rites, we invite abundance to flow through ourselves and our homes. Gratitude for the simple things, such as food, warmth, and family, brings forth many abundant treasures.

10 OF EARTH

Feeling: Prosperity, opulence, richness, gratitude, plenty, well-being, assets, securities, valuables, goods.

Ask yourself: What spiritual harvest will I collect at the end of this journey?

Action: Reflect on your failures and successes. Make sure to honor and celebrate the experience of it all.

Essence: When we celebrate what has been created through us, we know that the energy we put out will return back tenfold.

NOTES

Gray skies of autumn hover in stark contrast to the bright-yellow wheat fields and happy faces of the farmers. The joy and unity of the community can be witnessed at the annual Harvest Festival, which we lovingly call Obżynki. This Obżynki Festival is a time for celebration, when the abundant bounty of food and crops may be celebrated, giving thanks to Mother Nature for her generosity.

After the happy and carefree Kupala bonfire traditions faded, the harvest became a central focus for Ukrainian farmers. Harvesttime is one of the most dignified and fundamental periods of the year, since the well-being of each family depends on its results. No matter how hard the work in the field was, there were always cheerful, heart-led songs and soulful rituals that testify to the deep respect that our ancestors had for Mother Nature.

On the first eve of Obżynki, the owner of the farm or the oldest, most respected woman in the family solemnly prayed to the heavenly powers for mercy and support during the harvest season. They would cut the first bundle of grain stalks, known as a "harvest start," decorated with wildflowers and tied with red ribbon as a symbol of prosperity and well-being. With Spirit's blessing, the Obżynki begins. We call this "the Day of the First Sheaf."

At the end of the harvest season, the Obżynki Festival is held as a way to give thanks for the abundance that was given by the land and to ensure abundance for the next year's harvest. Traditional songs were performed, which glorified the hard labor of the Ukrainian people. A highlight of the ceremony was the choosing of a princess—a girl or a woman who distinguished herself during the harvest. They adorned the princess with the most magnificent wreath of ears of corn and flowers and accompanied her to the village with songs to begin Obżynki.

The last sheaf, known as Didukh,[1] was always collected in a group, because it is believed that the spirit of the field and abundance lived within it and that this spirit had the power to revive all the dead and increase the yield of all living things. It was respectfully brought home and kept until Christmas.

The Obżynki Festival is a celebration of the commitment, abundance, and gratitude that comes from living a righteous life. Choose your commitments and actions wisely, for these will certainly come back to you.

---

1. Didukh—2 of Air

Thank You

...for saying yes to the call & connection with this deck. Our hope is that this deck will help inspire you to create peace and love for humanity. And that you will find your Flower of the Magic Fern.

When you've had a chance to feel & connect with this deck,
please help us spread the love:
Take a photo of your favourite card, Post it to Social Media
& Tag Us @FLOWEROFTHEMAGICFERN

We will do a random draw for a 1 on 1 reading with the creator of this deck (Tania Andrushko) from those who have posted their favourite cards & tagged us.

For more information on this deck or any other services,
please visit www.taniaandrushko.com

GRATITUDE & ACKNOWLEDGMENTS

To my husband, Yuriy, who stood by me and held my hand. He who hugged me each time I retreated into my fears and stories and the old self-defeating question, "Who am I to do this?"

To my beautiful daughters, Anastasiia and Marta, who supported me in all ways they possibly could, including millions of you-have-this hugs.

To Helen and Masha, two souls who found the ways to represent the beauty, vibrancy, and magic of our native land through beautiful art and for magical telepathic collaboration with the ocean between us.

To Lisa, for your unwavering commitment, inquisitive mind, and endless curiosity to my culture and history.

To Steph, my dear friend who believes in me and inspires me with her cheerful laughter.

To Kim, for your solid trust and for being the first person to show up to support the creation of this material.

I am deeply grateful to Sam. There are no words to describe the love and appreciation I have for this shining soul.

Wes . . . and the song he wrote. This melody allowed me to see through the many layers of hesitation and doubt.

To my ancestors, who came and supported me by opening the historical books on the pages I needed and for showing me what is important to share and showcase from our history and culture.

To my grandmother Rosalia, who told me (from the sky above) to enjoy the process and not to worry since I am divinely guided.

To my grandfather Mykhola, whose beautiful singing voice (from the sky above) I heard each time I would encounter something that would bring the childhood memory to the surface. My raw emotions were soothed by his voice, even though he is not physically with me.

To my motherland Ukraine, who gave me my courage, energy, and assertiveness to become the person I am.

A Message from the Artist Mary

Hello, readers!

If you are here with me, then you may be wondering who is behind all these pictures that you see on the Tarot cards within this wonderful deck.

My name is Mary, and I'd love to tell you a little about myself. I was born and still live in Ukraine. I'm twenty-two years old and I have the dearest parents, a loving fiance, and an amazing cat, but I don't have my house anymore because we had to leave it due to the start of the war. I have been drawing since childhood and probably always wanted to connect my life with art, because for me it is the best way to communicate with the world.

Because of my experiences here in my homeland, everything I created together with Tania and Olena is very, very close to my heart. I tried to draw so that even people who do not know our culture could feel all its magic and beauty, which can be found in every detail.

When I first received the invitation to work on this project, I immediately in my heart felt that it was something special. When I found out that this is a project about Ukraine, for Ukraine, and with a Ukrainian soul, I didn't hesitate for a second. Why? Because I needed it so I would be inspired to keep living and holding on. I accepted this invitation because it is so important that the world learns about us, about Ukraine, about our beauty, soul, strength, art, history, and love. Right now, when it is so difficult for all of us, when we are fighting for our independence, when we stand to the last, when we might lose our homes, lose our families, lose faith in the future, this knowledge is tremendously important. And right now it is so important for the whole world to see the real us—bright, vibrant, courageous. These cards are the most beautiful, bright, and magical pieces of the Ukrainian soul, collected in a small box. I am sure that everyone who sees these cards at least once will feel it too. For that, I am thankful.

Working on this project was not easy, but it was very inspiring, with attention to every little detail and love at every touch. With Tania and Olena, we worked like a small family, becoming very close to each other. Their support, after another explosion in our city or another wave of terrible news, always helped me hang on, live, and move forward. I think that all the emotions and feelings that the war in our country evoked in me, I put into each drawing, so that I might dive headfirst into the peaceful, beautiful, multifaceted Ukraine, which forever leaves a mark in my heart. This project taught me to see beauty and hope, even when it seemed that there was nothing blooming and bright around me. It taught me to move forward, no matter what, for the sake of the common goal of creating something truly stunning such as this magical deck of cards.

I want to sincerely congratulate you, because it was you who became the owner of this deck of Tarot cards. Now this is the beginning of your own story!

With heartfelt gratitude,
Mary

A Message from the Artist Olena

Growing up in the beautiful city of Ivano-Frankivsk and spending some time at my grandma's village, I was always surrounded by the traditions and different festivities. Back then, everyday life was filled with craftsmanship, with people finding ways to make everything with their own hands. My grandfather had a workshop where he would carve wood to make all kinds of furniture pieces, and my grandmother would have these beautiful tablecloths and pillowcases that were carefully and intricately embroidered by her. A big part of my grandparents' lives was agriculture, and they spent so much time and effort growing everything themselves. The core of a Ukrainian spirit is creativity within, love for work, and celebration of each holiday with all the family and friends around, singing folk songs, remembering the meaning behind each holiday, and why it is important to celebrate it together. This always stood out in my memories of my grandparents and my home in Ukraine.

I learned many of the old traditions and forgotten songs at the music school I attended. Music and people's way of living were always intertwined through folk songs and music. We would have to reenact the old beliefs and certain folkloric events to commemorate our ancestors. It always sparked such a curiosity in me, since there was so much to discover.

When I moved to Canada, I felt uprooted, like a piece of me was left behind in my homeland. Part of me will always feel this way. However, this project opened up some new interest in me, digging deeper into the whole basis and foundation of how our culture was evolving and growing for centuries.

Hence, so much time, love, and research was put into this project to be accurate about the origins and meanings of every aspect of Ukrainian culture. To share the values that have been passed on to me, to give you another perspective on Ukrainian history and folklore, and to remind others why it is essential to look deep down into your roots and find yourself among them, no matter where you are from.

Let these cards help guide you along your path, find that inner purpose resting inside yourself, and treasure that magic flower that exists within you.

With love,
Olena